From
GRACE to
ETERNITY

To A beloved Neice
Joan Kalguee

From Aunt Dora &
Uncle John.

May you always
stay close to the
Lord

1-15-05

From GRACE to ETERNITY

Dana Howard Burnell

Pleasant Word

Packaged by Pleasant Word, PO Box 428, Enumclaw, WA 98022. The views expressed or implied in this work do not necessarily reflect those of Pleasant Word. The author(s) is ultimately responsible for the design, content and editorial accuracy of this work.

ISBN 1-4141-0063-9
Library of Congress Catalog Card Number: 2003114000

Contents

Prologue

I'm not a preacher. I'm not an eloquent public speaker or an inspirational writer. I am simply a student of God, an instrument for Him to play. As I began this work it was merely a compilation of the sermons I had the opportunity to present over the years. As I continued this work, I believed that it had to be more than a capture of isolated sermons. It needed to contain a thread that held it all together. Through my life the thread that has held me together is Jesus Christ. So this book is dedicated to Him. Its purpose is to help others to find, live, and share a fulfilled life in Christ. Its timeline is from the acceptance of God's gift of Christ, to our everlasting reward; "From Grace to Eternity." It is my prayer that as you read this book you will be moved towards a relationship with the Father, towards a life rich with meaning, and towards a compassion for the lost. To God be the glory.

I could not have finished this project without a fine crew of editors. Foremost is my wife, Kathryn. She has kept not only my book, but my life on track. Countless times I have passionately run the wrong way, finding myself stuck in a dead end alley, or helplessly circling a roundabout. Kathryn has helped me get back into the traffic of today. Her tireless editing and other work cannot be measured.

Clayton Boyce, Brad Perrigo, Bruce Pleasant, and Steve Sego from the Woodinville Church of Christ in Woodinville Washington were the men that validated my writing. Bruce and Steve I counted on to search the Scriptures to make sure that what I wrote was doctrinally sound and followed the Word of God. Clayton was there to lend his heart and make sure that God used me to tug at the heart strings of the reader. Everyone challenged me to make a difference with this book and to let Scripture speak boldly within its covers.

Finally, my greatest editor and foremost model for this book was our Savior, my Savior, Jesus Christ. It was from His Word that I drew my message, His inspiration that I drew my thoughts, and His heart that I drew my words. Without Him I would be nothing.

LOOKING TO BE SAVED

Many times people are reluctant to commit to a saving relationship with God through Christ. It's not an easy decision, nor is it one that should be made without a great deal of thought. When we put on Christ in baptism we're making a commitment. It's not fair to say that we are making the commitment of a lifetime, because it's more than that. We're making the commitment of a spiritual lifetime. We're making an eternal commitment. This is the biggest decision we will ever make. But it is the right decision. Without giving our lives to Christ, our name is not written in the Lambs Book of Life (Revelation 20:15) and we are dead in our sins (Ephesians 2:1–10).

There are, sadly, many excuses that people use to explain why they have never come to know Christ. All of these excuses can be divided into two categories. Either people choose not to follow Christ because the message seems too easy, or because the message seems too difficult.

The seriousness of the Gospel is that there are consequences for our belief or disbelief (John 3:18). The simplicity of the Gospel is that God sent His Son, Christ to die for you and I so that we might have eternal life in Heaven (John 3:16–17).

The reality is that every person who doesn't know Christ is kept from that relationship by bondage to sin. We are all lost (Matthew 18:12–14) and only a saving relationship with God through

Christ can save us. Repenting and committing to live a life for Christ is serious. We're giving our lives in service to someone, either Christ or Satan (Luke 16:13). Some people don't know God because the decision to follow Christ is not made. The default master is Satan. Just as Joshua had to choose to follow God (Joshua 24:15) we too have to choose to live for Christ. Failure to make this choice is failure to serve God.

We choose to follow someone whether we want to or not. We choose either out of loyalty, or complacency. Eternal reward or punishment awaits those whose choice is made intentionally (Romans 2:5–11). Those that choose not to choose are rewarded with punishment (Revelation 3:14–18).

Understanding the seriousness of the Gospel without understanding the entire message will cause people to loose heart. Understanding that we are lost in our sins, and separated from God (Ephesians 4:18), causes us to see the eternal hopelessness of our condition. Without knowing about a way of reconciliation, we often stop trying.

Understanding the grace of the Gospel without understanding the entire message will cause people to minimize its importance. Understanding only the loving story of the Gospel will lull people into believing that they're ok with an incomplete view of God. Youth, good fortune, popularity, great physical health, and other blessings combined with this incomplete understanding of God's relationship with man, can be huge stumbling blocks to a relationship with God. If we feel like we're in control, like life is wonderful, that we're invincible, and that we are loved by God, we're not too likely to see the separation that sin has caused between us and the Almighty.

Satan uses both of these incomplete understandings as tools for his work. For those that only see the love of God, Satan helps them to feel satisfied in their eternity. For those that see only the wrath of God, Satan helps them to feel helpless and apathetic.

This section is for those seeking to find God. It is for those with a humble heart that are ready to make a decision for Christ, live a changed life, and share in eternal salvation. It tries to tie together the seriousness of sin, and the grace of the Gospel, into a balanced understanding of the Christian commitment.

Chapter 1

The Serious message of Sin

The title to this chapter seems both appropriate and inappropriate at the same time. It is aptly titled because sin controls the world. Sin is the correct term to use when referring to many of the worlds pleasures, passions, and pastimes. Sin encompasses life around us every day, and if we are not careful and prayerful, we can easily be enticed into its folly. This chapter is inaptly named because although sin is real and lurking close by, the Blood of Jesus Christ is the antidote to sin, the armor of salvation, and the cleansing power of God. The severity of sin can be overcome by the power of Christ for those that believe and are faithful.

Sin, is separation from God. It is willfully doing things that are not in keeping with God's word. In

Matthew 7:21–23 Jesus tells us, "Not everyone who says to me, `Lord, Lord,' will enter the kingdom of heaven, but only he who does the will of my Father who is in heaven. Many will say to me on that day, `Lord, Lord, did we not prophesy in your name, and in your name drive out demons and perform many miracles?' Then I will tell them plainly, `I never knew you. Away from me, you evildoers!'" The key to that passage is "only he who does the will of my Father." Of course you need to be able to understand the will of God. Children, obviously cannot grasp the nature of God's will and are protected until such a time as they are intellectually mature enough to understand (Luke 18:15–17).

It's convicting when we look at Scripture and understand what God has defined as sinful. We see many examples of sin that we have or do indulge in, in a small way. In Matthew 5:33–37 Jesus again teaches us. It reads, "Again, you have heard that it was said to the people long ago, `Do not break your oath, but keep the oaths you have made to the Lord.' But I tell you, do not swear at all: either by heaven, for it is God's throne; or by the earth, for it is his footstool; or by Jerusalem, for it is the city of the Great King. And do not swear by your head, for you cannot make even one hair white or black. Simply let your `Yes' be `Yes,' and your `No,' `No'; anything beyond this comes from the evil one." This one simple passage convicts many of us. Almost all of us have had times where we have agreed to do something and have not fulfilled that agreement. Call it what you will, dishonesty or lying. Fudging on a promise to a child for a Saturday morning fishing trip, or cheating on your income taxes, are both equally sin in the eyes of God.

We try to water down the message of sin by putting mans desires ahead of God's. We say that Scripture was based on the customs of the day. We say that things are different today and "that passage" doesn't apply today. Hebrews 13:8 tells us that, "Jesus Christ is the same yesterday and today and forever." Instead of patterning our lives after Scripture, we want to change Scripture to justify our behavior. God does not change, and neither does His will.

Some of the issues that God plainly calls sin include: evil thoughts, murder, adultery, sexual immorality, theft, false testimony, slander (Matthew 15:19), greed, malice, deceit, lewdness, envy, arrogance, folly (Mark 7:21–22), orgies, drunkenness, debauchery, dissension, jealousy (Romans 13:13), idolatry, prostitution, homosexuality, greed, swindling (First Corinthians 6:9–10), impurity, witchcraft, hatred, discord, fits of rage, selfish ambition, factions (Galatians 5:19–20), any kind of impurity, obscenity, foolish talk, coarse joking (Ephesians 5:3–5), lust, evil desires (Colossians 3:5). This is just a partial list of things that God says will exclude you from those that go to Heaven.

But Sin is much more than a checklist of right and wrong. In Luke 18:18–22 Jesus portrays this to a young man. It reads, "A certain ruler asked him, 'Good teacher, what must I do to inherit eternal life?' 'Why do you call me good?' Jesus answered. 'No one is good—except God alone. You know the commandments: "Do not commit adultery, do not murder, do not steal, do not give false testimony, honor your father and mother."' 'All these I have kept since I was a boy,' he said. When Jesus heard this, he said to him, 'You still lack one thing. Sell everything you have and give to the poor, and you will have treasure in heaven. Then come, follow me.'" Sin is an attitude, a condition of the heart. Following Jesus is the key. Living a life with a heart that is turned towards Him is to live righteously. When the Jewish teachers of the law were questioning Jesus about the greatest commandment Jesus explained it all. In Matthew 22:35–40 we see, "One of them, an expert in the law, tested him with this question: 'Teacher, which is the greatest commandment in the Law?' Jesus replied: 'Love the Lord your God with all your heart and with all your soul and with all your mind. This is the first and greatest commandment. And the second is like it: Love your neighbor as yourself. All the Law and the Prophets hang on these two commandments.'" This passage sums up all of Christianity; a life lived for God.

Sin is also more powerful than we may imagine. Sin has a way of sucking us in. Sin begins in small steps, and grows stronger over time as we beat down our conscious and accustom ourselves to its presence. James 1:13–15 tells us, "When tempted, no one should say, 'God is tempting me.' For God cannot be tempted by evil, nor does he tempt anyone; but each one is tempted when, by his own evil desire, he is dragged away and enticed. Then, after desire has conceived, it gives birth to sin; and sin, when it is full-grown, gives birth to death." Sin is like a cancer; once it begins it flourishes and grows until it results in spiritual death. Romans 6:23 confirms this. It says, "For the wages of sin is death, but the gift of God is eternal life in Christ Jesus our Lord."

Romans 8:5–8 reads, "Those who live according to the sinful nature have their minds set on what that nature desires; but those who live in accordance with the Spirit have their minds set on what the Spirit desires. The mind of sinful man is death, but the mind controlled by the Spirit is life and peace; the sinful mind is hostile to God. It does not submit to God's law, nor can it do so. Those controlled by the sinful nature cannot please God." Sin starts off small, and grows to consume and control us.

Let me share a story with you.

A young Christian man opened his eyes and found himself embroiled in sin. His parents had a small store in Nebraska. They sold groceries, gasoline, tobacco products, alcohol, magazines, and other goods. The entrance to the store was a wide hallway with doors on either end leading to parking lots on both sides of the building. This young man worked at his parents store in the evenings. It was around this same time that Nebraska voted in a State Lottery. The lottery was funded with sales from scratch cards, and the introduction of computerized draw-poker gambling machines. It was the gambling machines that ended up the hallway of this store that got the young man into trouble. Or should I say the lack of self control when enticed by the machines that got him into trouble.

As the young man worked he watched as people came by and fed quarters to the draw-poker machines. Some won, but most lost. For some reason the young man found himself thinking he was luckier than most so he began to "dabble" with the machines. When he was at work and there weren't any customers in the store, he would spend a few dollars in quarters trying to win the jackpot. After a few days it became more than a couple of dollars. After a few weeks it became a problem.

After trying and loosing so often you would have thought the young man would have learned his lesson, but he did not. Eventually he began "borrowing" money from the register. This seemed fine so long as he won and paid it back before his shift was over. However it didn't always work that way. Eventually the young man found that he had pilfered more from the register than he could easily repay. He broke down with remorse when he realized that he was not only a gambler, but also had become a thief.

The young man went to his mother, confessed his transgressions and worked out a deal to repay her. Sin is enticing. It is engaging. It is entrapping. It is deadly.

When we look at ourselves with a checklist it may be easy to reason our way off the list of sinners. We may be able to convince ourselves that our motive was right when we told a "little white lie," or when we "weren't totally honest." But when we put it in perspective and hold our lives up to the light of Jesus, it's pretty easy to see our failings, to understand that we have not only sinned in our lives, but continue to sin today. Romans 3:23 tells us, "There is no difference, for all have sinned and fall short of the glory of God." The fact is, we are all sinners. Whether we tell a white lie, or steal from the register, sin is sin.

If all men have sinned, does that mean that God's creation was flawed? No! When God created mankind He created them perfectly. They were created in His image. Genesis 1:26–27 tells us, "Then God said, 'Let us make man in our image, in our likeness, and let them rule over the fish of the sea and the birds of the air, over the livestock, over all the earth, and over all the creatures that move along the ground.' So God created man in his own image, in the image of God he created him; male and female he created them."

God is holy and perfect, and desires all men to be holy and perfect as well. Matthew 5:48 says, "Be perfect, therefore, as your heavenly Father is perfect." First Peter 1:15–16 reads, "But just as he who called you is holy, so be holy in all you do; for it is written: 'Be holy, because I am holy.'"

So God created man in His image, perfect and holy. God created man as a thinking being with the ability to choose. God created us with free will. Genesis 2:8–17 shows us that free will. God gives a command that man has the option of obeying or not. These verses read, "Now the LORD God had planted a garden in the east, in Eden; and there he put the man he had formed. And the LORD God made all kinds of trees grow out of the ground—trees that were pleasing to the eye and good for food. In the middle of the garden were the tree of life and the tree of the knowledge of good and evil. A river watering the garden flowed from Eden; from there it was separated into four headwaters. The name of the first is the Pishon; it winds through the entire land of Havilah, where there is gold. (The gold of that land is good; aromatic resin and onyx are also there.) The name of the second river is the Gihon; it winds through the entire land of Cush. The name of the third river is the Tigris; it runs along the east side of Asshur. And the fourth river is the Euphrates. The LORD God took the man and put him in the Garden of Eden to work it and take care of it. And the LORD God commanded the man, 'You are free to eat from any tree in the garden; but you must not eat from the tree of the knowledge of good and evil, for when you eat of it you will surely die.'"

Satan was also alive and well and ready to turn man from his creator, God. Genesis 3:1–3 tells us, "Now the serpent was more crafty than any of the wild animals the LORD God had made. He said to the woman, 'Did God really say, "You must not eat from any tree in the garden?"' The woman said to the serpent, 'We may eat fruit from the trees in the garden, but God did say, "You must not eat fruit from the tree that is in the middle of the garden, and you must not touch it, or you will die."' 'You will not surely die,' the serpent said to the woman. 'For God knows that when you eat of it your eyes will be opened, and you will be like God, knowing good and evil.' When the woman saw that the fruit of the tree was good for food and pleasing to the eye, and also desirable for gaining wisdom, she took some and ate it. She also gave some to her husband, who was with her, and he ate it. Then the eyes of both of them were opened, and they realized they were naked; so they sewed fig leaves together and made coverings for themselves. Then the man and his wife heard the sound of the LORD God as he was walking in the garden in the cool of the day, and they hid from the LORD God among the trees of the garden. But the LORD God called to the man, 'Where are you?' He answered, 'I heard you in the garden, and I was afraid because I was naked; so I hid.' And he said, 'Who told you that you were naked? Have you eaten from the tree that I commanded you not to eat from?' The man said, 'The woman you put here with me—she gave me some fruit from the tree, and I ate it.' Then the LORD God said to the woman, 'What is this you have done?' The woman said, 'The serpent deceived me, and I ate.' So the LORD God said to the serpent, 'Because you have done this, Cursed are you above all the livestock and all the wild animals! You will crawl on your belly and you will eat dust all the days of your life. And I will put enmity between you and the woman, and between your offspring and hers; he will crush your head, and you will strike his heel.' To the woman he said, 'I will greatly increase your pains in childbearing; with pain you will give birth to children. Your desire will be for your husband, and he will rule over you.' To Adam he said, 'Because you listened to your wife and ate from the tree about which I commanded you, "You must not eat of it," Cursed is the ground because of you; through painful toil you will eat of it all the days of your life. It will produce thorns and thistles for you, and you will eat the plants of the field. By the sweat of your brow you will eat your food until you return to the ground, since from it you were taken; for dust you are and to dust you will return.' Adam named his wife Eve, because she would become the mother of all the living. The LORD God made garments of skin for Adam and his wife and clothed them. And the LORD God said, 'The man has now become like one of us, knowing good and evil. He must not be allowed to reach out his hand and take also from the tree of life and eat, and live forever.' So the LORD God banished him from the Garden of Eden to work the ground from which he had been taken. After he drove the man out, he placed on the east side of the Garden of Eden cherubim and a flaming sword flashing back and forth to guard the way to the tree of life."

So sin entered into the world through Adam. Adam and Eve ate from the tree of the knowledge of good and evil and sin entered into humanity. Romans 5:12–14 shows us that the image of God was tarnished when sin entered the world. It reads, "Therefore, just as sin entered the world through one man, and death through sin, and in this way death came to all men, because all sinned—for before the law was given, sin was in the world. But sin is not taken into account when there is no law. Nevertheless, death reigned from the time of Adam to the time of Moses, even over those who did not sin by breaking a command, as did Adam, who was a pattern of the one to come."

We are all guilty of sin. Sin came into the world because of disobedience to God and wrong choices. Sin is cancerous and consuming and eventually leads to spiritual death. What does it mean to reach spiritual death? Romans 1:18–25 reads, "The wrath of God is being revealed from heaven against all the godlessness and wickedness of men who suppress the truth by their wickedness, since what may be known about God is plain to them, because God has made it plain to them. For since the creation of the world God's invisible qualities—his eternal power and divine nature—have been clearly seen, being understood from what has been made, so that men are without excuse. For although they knew God, they neither glorified him as God nor gave thanks to him, but their thinking became futile and their foolish hearts were darkened. Although they claimed to be wise, they became fools and exchanged the glory of the immortal God for images made to look like mortal man and birds and animals and reptiles. Therefore God gave them over in the sinful desires of their hearts to sexual impurity for the degrading of their bodies with one another. They exchanged the truth of God for a lie, and worshiped and served created things rather than the Creator—who is forever praised. Amen."

Spiritual death is being on the outside of a relationship with God. When Christ returns (Matthew 24:30–31) we will be judged. Romans 2:5–11 tells us that those that are living sinful lives are subject to the wrath and anger of God. It reads, "But because of your stubbornness and your unrepentant heart, you are storing up wrath against yourself for the day of God's wrath, when his righteous judgment will be revealed. God will give to each person according to what he has done. To those who by persistence in doing good seek glory, honor and immortality, he will give eternal life. But for those who are self-seeking and who reject the truth and follow evil, there will be wrath and anger. There will be trouble and distress for every human being who does evil: first for the Jew, then for the Gentile; but glory, honor and peace for everyone who does good: first for the Jew, then for the Gentile. For God does not show favoritism." Spiritual death is not just being outside of a relationship with God, it's to endure His wrath and anger.

Matthew 25:31–46 tells us, "When the Son of Man comes in his glory, and all the angels with him, he will sit on his throne in heavenly glory. All the nations will be gathered before him, and he will separate the people one from another as a shepherd separates the sheep from the goats. He will put the sheep on his right and the goats on his left. Then the King will say to those on his right, `Come, you who are blessed by my Father; take your inheritance, the kingdom prepared for you since the creation of the world. For I was hungry and you gave me something to eat, I was thirsty and you gave me something to drink, I was a stranger and you invited me in, I needed clothes and you clothed me, I was sick and you looked after me, I was in prison and you came to visit me.' Then the righteous will answer him, `Lord, when did we see you hungry and feed you, or thirsty and give you something to drink? When did we see you a stranger and invite you in, or needing clothes and clothe you? When did we see you sick or in prison and go to visit you?' The King will reply, `I tell you the truth, whatever you did for one of the least of these brothers of mine, you did for me.' Then he will say to those on his left, `Depart from me, you who are cursed, into the eternal fire prepared for the devil and his angels. For I was hungry and you gave me nothing to eat, I was thirsty and you gave me nothing to drink, I was a stranger and you did not invite me in, I needed clothes and you did not clothe me, I was sick and in prison and you did not look after me.' They also will answer, `Lord, when did we see you hungry or thirsty or a stranger or needing clothes or sick or in prison, and did not help you?' He will reply, `I tell you the truth, whatever you did not do for one of the least of these, you did not do for me.' Then they will go away to eternal punishment, but the righteous to eternal life." Spiritual death is being on the outside of a relationship with God. It's enduring His wrath and anger. It's eternal punishment. It's a place called Hell.

Sin, controlling and growing is truly a difficult message. Understanding the evil behind it and knowing that we are all enticed and lead astray by its power is a scary thing. Scarier still is the outcome of a sinful life. Separation from God, subjection to His wrath and anger, and destined to an eternity in Hell. These are pretty sobering thoughts.

As in Acts 2:37, the people who heard the first sermon preached in the New Testament Church responded, we need to ask ourselves the question, "Brothers, what shall we do?" How do we escape the bondage of sin and the eternal punishment that awaits? This question is the sum total of the seriousness of sin. To find the answer, keep reading. It's in the second chapter.

Let me share a poem with you.

"Death Through Sin" by Dana H. Burnell

Sin is a little thing when we give it birth, Just some slight bending of God's precious Word. Nothing too sinister, evil or vile, and we plan to partake of it, just for a while.

Sin is a medium thing, as it starts to grow, first only inward, but now it starts to show, a little less character, a little less sure, not quite as steady and not quite as pure.

Sin becomes larger, as it takes our life, it brings to our world, unbelievable strife. As it overtakes us, it tears us away, from our Lord and our Father, who want us to stay.

At judgment we kneel to the author of life, and He looks at our record, our sin and our strife. If the record exists, to his left we will go, "Depart from me," He'll say, "for you I don't know." If the records been washed by Christ's blood then we win, and the Lord of the Cross will say, "Come, enter in."

"Therefore, since we are surrounded by such a great cloud of witnesses, let us throw off everything that hinders and the sin that so easily entangles, and let us run with perseverance the race marked out for us. Let us fix our eyes on Jesus, the author and perfecter of our faith, who for the joy set before him endured the cross, scorning its shame, and sat down at the right hand of the throne of God. Consider him who endured such opposition from sinful men, so that you will not grow weary and lose heart (Hebrews 12:1–3)."

Chapter 2

The Simple Message of the Gospel

*H*ave you ever worked with youngsters as they searched for the Truth? How old do they need to be before they can have a trusting relationship with God through Christ? Eight? Ten? Twelve? How mature do they need to be? How much of the Bible do they need to fully understand? How many Scriptures do they need to have memorized? While all of the above are great things to help us gain a better understanding of our Lord, they are not necessarily prerequisites to salvation. You do need to be old enough to be accountable for your actions. You do need to be mature enough to understand the gravity and seriousness of the commitment you make to live a Godly life. You do need to fully understand the relationship that you are putting on with Christ. You don't need to have memorized any Scripture. You don't need to be a Bible scholar. You don't need to understand religious history. The point of this chapter is that we need not be the smartest, most educated, most outstanding individuals to become Christians. The gospel message is not profound beyond understanding. God has made His message simple, and salvation is the free gift of God for anyone that chooses to accept it.

The world would have us believe that the gospel message is difficult to understand. It would have us believe that the effort required to become a Christian is more than we can bear. Satan uses these misconceptions to keep us away from God. The reality is that God has laid the foundation of our relationship with Him, through Christ (Ephesians 2:19–20). He did all the work. He is offering salvation to all who accept it. Many times there are stumbling blocks that get in the way of forming the right relationship with God. These either come because our sin has us convinced that we're comfortable where we are, or convinced that we're ok where we are, or because we're afraid that somehow we are too sinful, or too ignorant, or too plain to be a child of God.

Have you ever really looked at the entirety of the plan of God for the salvation of Man? Have you ever considered the plan that God laid out from before the foundation of the world? John 1:1–5 tells us, "In the beginning was the Word, and the Word was with God, and the Word was God. He was with God in the beginning. Through him all things were made; without him nothing was made that has been made. In him was life, and that life was the light of men. The light shines in the darkness, but the darkness has not understood it." This is a plan in which there is a lot of work to be done. This is a plan which takes centuries to unfold. This is a plan through which peoples' hearts are touched for generations. This is a plan through which God has shouldered the burden, and man is receiving the benefits. Man's part in this miraculous equation is simple and easy to follow.

Before we can look at what we must do to be saved, we first need to examine God's part of man's salvation. After that we will look at the things that we tend to put in the way of our development of a saving relationship with God. Finally, we will look at man's part of the relationship, or as the men said to Peter at Pentecost, "What must we do to be saved (Acts 2:37)?"

I don't think it is fair to say that God's part in salvation is hard, not for God, but it is fair to say that it required a great deal of effort on His part. Everything that we know about God, everything He has revealed to us through Scripture, and all that He has shown us through the world around us, points to the fact that God did it all for His creation, mankind.

Let's look at God's work. For starters God created the world, the heavens, and the earth. He worked out all of the details of the existence of living things, both plants and animals. This creation included atoms and molecules, fit together to make rocks and trees, water and earth. It included stars and sunlight, time and space. The work of God's creation is indescribable. We can read about the creation account in the first chapter of Genesis. After God created this wonderful world, universe, and all that comprise them, so that man would be comfortable, God created man. Genesis 2:7 reads, "Then the Lord God formed man of the dust of the ground, and breathed into his nostrils the breath of life, and man became a living being." Verses 20:–24 read, "And the man gave names to all the cattle, and to the birds of the sky, and to every beast of the field, but for Adam, there was not found a helper suitable for him. So the Lord God caused a deep sleep to fall upon the man, and he slept; then He took one of his ribs and closed up the flesh at that place. And the Lord God fashioned into a woman, the rib which He had taken from the man, and brought her to the man. And the man said, 'This is now bone of my bones, and flesh of my flesh, she shall be called woman because she was taken out of man.' For this cause a man shall leave his father and mother and shall cleave to his wife and they shall become one flesh." So God made this place for us to live, in all its wonder and glory. Then He created all the plants and animals. Then He created man. And so that man would not be alone, God created woman as his companion and helpmate. Mankind was complete.

But God wasn't yet done with His plan for man. He knew that man was frail and weak. He knew that we would fall before the temptations of sin, and draw away from Him unless He was able to teach us, and reach us. So He created the Law, and He passed it on to Moses. He created the law so that we could see our need for a Savior, for as Paul states in Galatians 3:24, "Therefore the Law has become our tutor to lead us to Christ that we may be justified by faith." God created the Law to act as a tutor to help man learn about our inability to overcome sin on our own. He created the Law to help us understand our need for His saving relationship freely offered to us through faith in Christ.

But God was still not done. God then gave us His greatest gift of all. We see in the very familiar passage of John 3:16, "God so loved the world that He gave His only begotten Son, that whoso-ever shall believe in Him, should not perish, but have eternal life." God, after creating the heavens and the earth, creating mankind, and showing him vividly through the Law, that he was separated from God by sin, unable to bridge the gap, came to earth as Christ Jesus, to be our example, to be our sacrifice, to show us the way to Heaven, and to pay for our sins.

And then, that we might have faith, and believe in all of it, He raised Jesus from the dead (Ephesians 1:17, 20–22). He did this so that Satan might be overcome, our sins might be forgiven and forgotten, and that we might believe.

God went through a lot of work, over a long period of time because of His love for man. He created and guided, and to this day, holds it all together (Colossians 1:16–17). God is still at work for us.

And through His wondrous plan, He made it so incredibly easy for man. Salvation for man, through faith in God is not burdensome. It's easy, and it's simple.

Many organizations or groups have membership requirements, prerequisites to becoming members. Some require you to pass IQ tests. Others require you to donate money. Several groups require that you pass the scrutiny of voting by some board or governing body. We however are much more subtle in our approach. As Christians we build roadblocks by ourselves, roadblocks more eternal, than the requirements raised by other groups as mentioned above. These become roadblocks to our salvation.

We tend to make rules that base our salvation on our knowledge, and our understanding of New Testament Scriptures, or of our knowing all the answers. Look at the Ethiopian eunuch in Acts 8:26–

39, "But an Angel of the Lord spoke to Phillip saying, 'Arise and go south to the road that descends from Jerusalem to Gaza.' And he arose and went; and behold, there was an Ethiopian eunuch, a court official of Candace, queen of the Ethiopians, who was in charge of all her treasure; and he had come to Jerusalem to worship. And he was returning and sitting in his chariot, and was reading the prophet Isaiah. And the Spirit said to Phillip, 'Go up and join this chariot.' And when Phillip had run up, he heard him reading Isaiah the prophet, and said, 'Do you understand what you are reading?' And he said, 'Well how could I, unless someone guides me?' And he invited Phillip to come up and sit with him. Now the passage of Scripture he was reading was this: 'He was led as a sheep to slaughter; and as a lamb before its sheerer was silent so he does not open his mouth. In humiliation his judgment was taken away; who shall relate his generation? For his life is removed from the earth.' And the eunuch answered Philip and said, 'Please tell me, of whom does the prophet say this? Of himself or of someone else?' And Philip opened his mouth, and beginning from this Scripture, he preached Jesus to him. And as they went along the road they came to some water; and the eunuch said, 'Look! Water! What prevents me from being baptized?' And Philip said, 'If you believe with all your heart you may.' And he answered and said, 'I believe that Jesus Christ is the Son of God.' And he ordered the chariot to stop; and they both went down into the water; Philip as well as the eunuch, and he baptized him. And when they came up out of the water, the Spirit of the Lord snatched Philip away; and the eunuch saw him no more, but went on his way rejoicing."

This man didn't have the New Testament to study, it hadn't even been written then. He didn't know all the answers either. I don't want to downplay the eunuch's relationship with God. He was a Godly man, and his traveling from Ethiopia to Jerusalem to worship was a testimony to his devout faith. But what he learned about Christ, the way he put the pieces together, came about through a single encounter with Phillip. In this one encounter he heard the gospel, believed and stated his belief in Christ as the Son of God, repented, and was joined with God's family through baptism. This is not to say that we shouldn't mature, and learn the word of God, we surely should, but the gift of Salvation doesn't demand that we understand it all. It isn't how much you know but the sincerity of your heart that leads to salvation.

We also tend to burden salvation with compensation. We say, well I don't have enough time, or I don't have any money to give to the Church. We make what we can give a pre-requisite to salvation. We know that giving is important. As Paul wrote in Second Corinthians 9:7, "Each man should give what he has decided in his heart to give, not reluctantly or under compulsion, for God loves a cheerful giver." The mistake that we make is that we convince ourselves that we haven't done enough to be saved. The reality is that no matter how hard you try, you cannot buy or work your way into salvation. In Second Timothy 1:8–10, Paul says, "So do not be ashamed to testify about our Lord, or ashamed of me his prisoner. But join with me in suffering for the gospel, by the power of God, who has saved us and called us to a holy life—not because of anything we have done but because of his own purpose and grace. This grace was given us in Christ Jesus before the beginning of time, but it has now been revealed through the appearing of our Savior, Christ Jesus, who has destroyed death and has brought life and immortality to light through the gospel."

We put sin in the way of Salvation. We tend to believe that unless we stop all of our sins and become white as snow, we cannot be saved. Repentance is indeed a part of our acceptance of God's grace. Repentance is a turning away from the evil of sin and turning towards God. Accepting Jesus means that you're heart is changed, and your actions will follow, but it's not immediate deliverance from years of practiced bad habits. As Christians we come up out of the waters of baptism with a gift that helps us to overcome sin. God gives believers the gift of the indwelling of His Holy Spirit when we are baptized. In the second chapter of Acts God's Church is established. As Peter finished the first recorded New Testament sermon, the crowd asks how to receive salvation, and Peter tells them in verse 38, "Repent and be baptized, every one of you, in the name of Jesus Christ for the forgiveness of your sins. And you will receive the gift of the Holy Spirit." As sinners we develop bad habits, our charge is to develop good habits in replacement of the bad. We don't come up out of the water of baptism immediately removed of our old sinful habits, but immediately cleansed and perfected, so that our those habits are no longer are held against us. The mistake is that we tell ourselves that we have to be perfect before we commit to a life with Christ. Instead we need to realize that we are perfected as we enter that life.

God has done a lot. His part of the plan for man is wonderfully engineered, and flawlessly executed; even when we try to get in the way. But if this plan is so simple for man, what exactly does man have to do?

There are five things that must occur in order for a person to be saved. None of these, in-and-of themselves provide salvation, but these events or actions, when joined together in the faithful heart, allow us to accept the free gift of God's grace. This is the transformation of salvation. Romans 12:2 tells us, "Do not conform any longer to the pattern of this world, but be transformed by the renewing of your mind. Then you will be able to test and approve what God's will is—his good, pleasing and perfect will."

The first thing that has to happen is that we need to hear the Gospel. We need to hear about the death, burial, and resurrection of Jesus Christ, the Son of God. Romans 10:14–15 asks, "How, then, can they call on the one they have not believed in? And how can they believe in the one of whom they have not heard?" It is certain that we cannot become one with Christ if we have never heard of Him.

The second thing that must happen is that we must believe in that gospel. We need to believe with all our hearts that Christ is the Son of God. In the gospel of John, chapter three, starting in verse 16 it reads, "For God so loved the world that he gave his one and only Son, that whoever believes in him shall not perish but have eternal life. For God did not send his Son into the world to condemn the world, but to save the world through him. Whoever believes in him is not condemned, but whoever does not believe stands condemned already because he has not believed in the name of God's one and only Son."

What does it mean to believe? We need to be totally convinced that Jesus Christ is the Son of the living God. Believe with your heart. In the story of Phillip and the Eunuch (Acts chapter eight), Phillip says, "If you believe with ALL of your heart." That, I think is a stumbling block for many. I think there are two parts to this idea of belief, the first is the belief itself, and the second is the depth of that belief.

Jesus emphasized the idea that we need to become like little children if we are going to receive salvation. Matthew chapter 18 tells this story. It reads, "At that time, the disciples came to Jesus saying, 'Who then is greatest in the kingdom of heaven?' And He called a child to Himself and set him before them, and said, 'Truly I say to you, unless you are converted and become like children, you shall not enter the kingdom of heaven. Whoever then humbles himself as this child, he is the greatest in the kingdom of heaven.'"

We need to understand the idea of believing in faith. We tend to want to know all the answers, and use terms like "prove it to me", but the kind of belief that God wants us to have for salvation is not something that can be proven by history. We have not experienced Heaven before. This belief is a belief stemming from our faith.

In John 20:19–29 we see the story of Thomas. It reads, "When therefore it was evening, on that day, the first day of the week, and when the doors were shut where the disciples were for fear of the Jews, Jesus came and stood in their midst, and said to them, 'Peace be with you.' And when He had said this, He showed them both His hands and His side. The disciples therefore rejoiced when they saw the Lord. Jesus therefore said to them again, 'Peace be with you; As the Father has sent Me, I also send you.' And when He had said this He breathed on them, and said to them, 'Receive the Holy Spirit. If you forgive the sins of any, their sins have been forgiven them; if you retain the sins of any, they have been retained.' But Thomas, one of the twelve called Didymus, was not with them when Jesus came. The other disciples were therefore saying to him, 'We have seen the Lord.' But he said to them, 'Unless I shall see in His hands the imprint of the nails, and put my hand into His side, I will not believe.' And after eight days again, His disciples were inside and Thomas with them. Jesus came, the doors having been shut, and stood in their midst, and said, 'Peace be with you.' Then He said to Thomas, 'Reach here your finger and see my hands; and reach here your hand and put it into my side; and be not unbelieving, but believing.' Thomas answered and said to Him, 'My Lord and my God.' Jesus said to him, 'Because you have seen me, you have believed? Blessed are they who did not see and yet believed.'" This is really what it means to believe. To believe without seeing, to believe without absolute proof, to believe with all our heart, is the kind of belief that God wants us to have.

In 1943 Reinhold Neibuhr penned, what has become known as the serenity prayer. It goes like this, "God give us grace to accept with sincerity the things that cannot be changed, courage to change the things that should be changed, and the wisdom to distinguish the one from the other." This understanding of what needs to be changed and the courage to change it is really the basis for the next piece of this salvation transformation.

The outcome of someone hearing and believing in the word of God will be a repentant heart. This is the next piece of the transformation of our hearts that happens through faith in God's grace. As we saw earlier from Acts 2:39, Peter charged those who wanted to be saved to repent. Repentance is a turning away from the nature of sin, and turning towards God. Romans 3:23 shows us that, "all have sinned and fallen short of the Glory of God." Repentance is necessary for everyone. Those who are good people leading good lives need to repent as much as the outrageously evil, who have committed the vilest of sin. Sin is sin in God's eyes. In Ephesians 2:1–3, Paul writes, "As for you, you were dead in your transgressions and sins, in which you used to live when you followed the ways of this world and of the ruler of the kingdom of the air, the spirit who is now at work in those who are disobedient. All of us also lived among them at one time, gratifying the cravings of our sinful nature and following its desires and thoughts." We all have sinned, and need to repent. We need to turn our hearts from the world, and towards God.

The next thing that must occur is that the convicted, believing, repentant heart will want to confess the name of Jesus. In Matthew 10:32, Jesus says, "Whoever acknowledges me before men, I will also acknowledge him before my Father in heaven" Romans 10:9 tells us that, "That if you confess with your mouth, 'Jesus is Lord,' and believe in your heart that God raised him from the dead, you will be saved." Sometimes we are reticent to talk about things in front of other people, especially things that are personal in nature.

Let me share a story with you.

I once was affiliated with a multi-level marketing insurance and mutual fund company. The idea was that if you hire people to do this with you, you get a cut of their commissions. I really believed that this was a great opportunity where I could make a difference in the lives of my family and others. I believed this so strongly that I convinced 45 people over a two month period to join this organization and become insurance evangelists. I was not afraid to speak to anyone about this opportunity. That's because I had this level of belief in the company.

That story illustrates the depth of commitment that God wants us to have in Christ. If we truly believe that Christ is the Son of God, proclaiming that fact will not be hard to do. In fact it will be hard to keep ourselves from proclaiming it to everyone we meet.

The final culmination of our conversion is the obedient act of baptism. Acts 2:38 shows us that baptism is when we are forgiven of our sins, and when we receive the gift of the Holy Spirit. As I noted at the beginning of this chapter, none of these steps alone will lead to salvation. Baptizing a person who hasn't repented or doesn't believe in Christ as the Son of God does nothing more than to get them wet.

Baptism is probably the biggest stumbling block that man makes for himself. It is also one of the greatest tools that Satan has to keep men from God. Many verses in Scripture talk about different parts of the salvation transformation, but none speak of them all together. It's logical to understand that we must hear about Jesus before we can believe in Him. It's logical to understand that we must believe in Him before we will confess His name, and turn our lives towards Him in repentance. These are really the toughest things for man to overcome. Baptism is necessary for salvation. It is easy for a changed heart to understand, desire, and complete. It's the point at which we are clothed in Christ (Galatians 3:26–27). It's the point at which we receive our salvation (First Peter 3:21). It is the magnum opus of our conversion transformation.

God is so awesome! He went to all the work to create all that is so that mankind could be comfortable. He created mankind, both man and woman. He created the law in order to teach us about our sinful, lost, condition, and our inability to change it. Then He sent His Son, a part of the Godhead, to humble Himself and come to earth. He sent His Son to live as an example, and to die as a sacrifice. God did all this because of His love for us!

Our part to salvation is so simple that we make up our own obstacles. All we need to do is accept through faith with a sincere believing, repentant heart, the gift that God offers. That's what we need to teach our children and those around us. We need to simply take God's hand and accept His Gift.

Let me share a poem with you.

"My Transformation" by Dana H. Burnell

I knew of the Bible when I was a child.
I knew "Jesus Loves Me," I sang it and smiled.
I knew that Christ lived, and that God was His
    dad,
But that's the extent of the knowledge I had.
I hadn't digested the fullness of God,
or the gift of His Son, or the paths that He trod.
I wasn't convinced of my guilt for my sin,
And Gods Holy Spirit had never come in.

But God sent a messenger into my life,
She taught me the Gospel, and then was my wife.
I heard the whole story, of how sin leads to death,
and how God's gift of mercy, is our saving breath.
I believed in the fact that Christ came as a man,
who through death freely opened, the gates to
    God's plan.
I believed in His mercy and my death due to sin,

I accepted His offer, and invited Him in.

I turned from my old ways, in all that I could,
In all that I learned and that I understood.
I gave up some old friends, and challenged my
heart,
To be sure that I wanted this race from the start.
I was baptized in water, submersed all in all,
And God graciously answered my souls aching
call.
My sins were forgiven, and the Spirit came in,
For the first time in my life, the race I could
win.

If you haven't put on Christ in baptism, wait no longer. You don't need to know everything; you don't need to understand everything. You simply need to believe with all your heart that Jesus is the Son of the living God and confess Him before men. Then you can be baptized into His death, burial, and resurrection receiving the Gift of the Holy Spirit. You can then begin your walk with God.

Chapter 3

Balancing God

*T*wo things that always seem to come out when I preach are my firm belief that people need to have their own individual active faith in God, and the fact that Scripture shows one Gospel. It shows one plan for man that God created before the formation of the world. A plan that is still active and orchestrated today by God.

These same two ideas have been around for centuries, but because of our stubborn nature, many of us still fail to hit the mark in establishing a relationship with God that is the kind of relationship that He wants us to have with Him. We tend to establish the kind of relationship that we want. A relationship in which we feel justified, or exonerated. A relationship that gives us confidence and reduces our nagging conscience.

Let me share a story with you.

When I was grade school we had a principal named Mrs. Flarity. I remember her as being a sweet old lady with a round face that always had a smile. She was a large lady, tall by a fifth-graders standards. There was a time when some of the other children were picking on me at recess and she defended me. I thought she was the greatest. Another time, however I got caught throwing rocks on the playground and was sent to her office. I was amazed at how mean she could be. She scolded me and lectured me on the danger of throwing rocks. She even called my mom! I didn't understand at such a tender age that Mrs. Flarity had both the job of being the justice of the peace, and the ambassador of good will. She had to discipline and care for her students.

As easy as it may be now as an adult to understand Mrs. Flarity's role, God's role is infinitely more complex. We can never truly understand God, because He is so awesome and mighty, and we so mortal and frail. We can never truly understand the power that He has. But He has given us something to help. He has given us His biography of sorts, His Word, Scripture, the Bible, so that we may fully understand everything He wants us to know of Him.

The book of Job is one of my favorite books of the Old Testament because it gives us such a graphic picture of the awesome power of God. In chapter 38 starting in verse 22 we read, "Have you entered the storehouses of the snow or seen the storehouses of the hail, which I reserve for times of trouble, for days of war and battle? What is the way to the place where the lightning is dispersed, or the place where the east winds are scattered over the earth? Who cuts a channel for the torrents of rain, and a path for the thunderstorm, to water a land where no man lives, a desert with no one in it, to satisfy a desolate wasteland and make it sprout with grass? Does the rain have a father? Who fathers the drops of dew? From whose womb comes the ice? Who gives birth to the frost from the heavens when the waters become hard as stone, when the surface of the deep is frozen?"

"Can you bind the beautiful Pleiades? Can you loose the cords of Orion? Can you bring forth the constellations in their seasons or lead out the Bear with its cubs? Do you know the laws of the heavens? Can you set up God's dominion over the earth?"

"Can you raise your voice to the clouds and cover yourself with a flood of water? Do you send the lightning bolts on their way? Do they report to you, `Here we are'? Who endowed the heart with wisdom or gave understanding to the mind? Who has the wisdom to count the clouds? Who can tip over the water jars of the heavens when the dust becomes hard and the clods of earth stick together?"

Scripture definitely paints for us a picture of a God that is omnipotent and omniscient. All powerful, and all knowing. Scripture also tells us that this book is everything we need to know to be good stewards for God. Second Timothy 3:16 tells us. "All Scripture is God-breathed and is useful for teaching, rebuking, correcting and training in righteousness, so that the man of God may be thoroughly equipped for every good work."

Thoroughly equipped. Lacking nothing. Understanding fully, everything we need to know.

So the problem in our lack of understanding of God is not God's fault, because He has given us all of the tools that we need. It's our fault. God revealed everything about Himself that we need to know to have a right relationship with Him. The problem is that we tend to look one way or the other and see a God that meets our own needs, a God that caters to our own selfish desire to be comfortable in what we choose to believe. We choose our beliefs, they do not choose us. You may argue that you don't believe one thing or another but every individual makes choices that define their set of beliefs. We tend to have a very kind of "Heads or Tails" understanding of God. Taking the things that suite the way we want to believe, and ignoring the things that make us uncomfortable. We fail sometimes to realize that as Luke said, the Kingdom of Heaven is like a precious coin (Luke 15:8), and that coin has more than one side. In this chapter I want to look the two major differences in the way that people see God, and try to determine how we balance the two to get an accurate picture of our Creator.

The first side of the coin that we tend to look at is our understanding of the God of love and grace. This is a very easy pill for us to swallow. First John 4:16 tells us that "God is love." We are familiar with lots of passages about love in Scripture. And from these, we can learn a lot about the nature of God and what He means when He uses the term love.

In First Corinthians, chapter 13, verses 4–13 we read, "love is patient, love is kind. It does not envy, it does not boast, it is not proud. It is not rude, it is not self-seeking, it is not easily angered, it keeps no record of wrongs. Love does not delight in evil but rejoices with the truth. It always protects, always trusts, always hopes, always perseveres. Love never fails. But where there are prophecies, they will cease; where there are tongues, they will be stilled; where there is knowledge, it will pass away. For we know in part and we prophesy in part, but when perfection comes, the imperfect disappears. When I was a child, I talked like a child, I thought like a child, I reasoned like a child. When I became a man, I put childish ways behind me. Now we see but a poor reflection as in a mirror; then we shall see face to face. Now I know in part; then I shall know fully, even as I am fully known. And now these three remain: faith, hope and love. But the greatest of these is love."

So the love of God is the goodness that we find in other people, the warm fuzzy things that make us happy and joyous and fill our hearts. And that is exactly how Scripture portrays God, as a God of love and mercy. God said to Moses in Exodus 33:19, "I will have mercy on whom I will have mercy, and I will have compassion on whom I will have compassion."

God has made a definite choice to be a loving and compassionate God. It isn't an accident. He says that He will have mercy on whom He wills to have mercy.

He created a plan for our salvation, and then He brought Jesus into the world to teach us about His love. In Jesus example of giving Himself up to death on the cross, we can see the Love of God as never seen before. We can see in the very familiar passage of John 3:16 "For God so loved the world that He gave His one and only Son, that whoever believes in Him shall not perish but have eternal life. For God did not send His Son into the world to condemn the world, but to save the world through Him." God truly loves us. He has given everything for us.

Jesus, while on earth taught us of the love of God. He said that the greatest commandments were these; to Love the Lord your God with all of your heart and soul and strength and mind, and to love your neighbor as yourself (Mark 12:30–31).

In looking at the things that Christ endured towards the end of His life, we see that He was beaten, mocked, ridiculed, spat upon, scourged, crucified and killed, and still while hanging on the cross He could say, "Father forgive them, for they do not know what they have done (Luke 23:34)." This is truly a picture of a God of Love.

Earlier in the chapter we noted that First John 4:6 tells us that "God is Love." But just a little bit earlier in First John 3:16 it says, "This is how we know what love is: Jesus Christ laid down his life for us." If God is Love, this is how we know what God is, through the love that He portrayed by sending Christ to die for us.

And not only that, God has created a great and glorious place for us to spend eternity with Him. It's a place called Heaven. Revelation 21 shows us a picture of this place. In this chapter we read the following, "One of the seven angels who had the seven bowls full of the seven last plagues came and said to me, 'Come, I will show you the bride, the wife of the Lamb.' And he carried me away in the Spirit to a mountain great and high, and showed me the Holy City, Jerusalem, coming down out of heaven from God. It shone with the glory of God, and its brilliance was like that of a very precious jewel, like a jasper, clear as crystal. It had a great, high wall with twelve gates and with twelve angels at the gates. On the gates were written the names of the twelve tribes of Israel. There were three gates on the east, three on the north, three on the south and three on the west. The wall of the city had twelve foundations, and on them were the names of the twelve apostles of the Lamb."

"The angel who talked with me had a measuring rod of gold to measure the city, its gates and its walls. The city was laid out like a square, as long as it was wide. He measured the city with the rod and found it to be 12,000 stadia (a stadia is about 202 yards) in length, and as wide and high as it is long. He measured its wall and it was 144 cubits thick, by man's measurement, which the angel was using. The wall was made of jasper, and the city of pure gold, as pure as glass. The foundations of the city walls were decorated with every kind of precious stone. The first foundation was jasper, the second sapphire, the third chalcedony, the fourth emerald, the fifth sardonyx, the sixth carnelian, the seventh chrysolite, the eighth beryl, the ninth topaz, the tenth chrysoprase, the eleventh jacinth, and the twelfth amethyst. The twelve gates were twelve pearls, each gate made of a single pearl. The great street of the city was of pure gold, like transparent glass."

I did not see a temple in the city, because the Lord God Almighty and the Lamb are its temple. The city does not need the sun or the moon to shine on it, for the glory of God gives it light, and the Lamb is its lamp."

God truly is a God of love and mercy. We serve an awesome God, willing and able to forgive us, strengthen us, help us, guide us, care for us, and even send His Son to die for us. This is the God that Scripture portrays. A loving and gracious God. A God that has planned for us, planted us, cared for us, nurtured us, and prepared for eternity with us.

But remember, God's attributes, and eternity are like both sides of the coin. There is another side of God portrayed in Scripture. The vengeful God.

In Jeremiah 42: God said to the Israelites, "This is what the LORD Almighty, the God of Israel, says: `As my anger and wrath have been poured out on those who lived in Jerusalem, so will my wrath be poured out on you when you go to Egypt. You will be an object of cursing and horror, of condemnation and reproach; you will never see this place again.'"

God is also a God of anger and wrath. Now before I continue down this path, and because of our one-sided view of God, I feel I need to explain, that even though Scripture depicts God with this nature, God is still pure, Holy, and totally Good. It's the holiness and justness of God that causes Him to act with vengeance towards people when they commit sin.

In Genesis 3:23–24 we read where God sent Adam and Eve from the Garden. "So the LORD God banished him from the Garden of Eden to work the ground from which he had been taken. After He drove the man out, He placed on the east side of the Garden of Eden cherubim and a flaming sword flashing back and forth to guard the way to the tree of life."

We also see where God destroyed the earth with a flood. In Genesis chapter six, verses 11–13, it reads, "Now the earth was corrupt in God's sight and was full of violence. God saw how corrupt the earth had become, for all the people on earth had corrupted their ways. So God said to Noah, 'I am going to put an end to all people, for the earth is filled with violence because of them. I am surely going to destroy both them and the earth.'" And we know that it rained for 40 days and 40 nights and all of the world's people were destroyed except for Noah and his family.

We also know the story of Sodom and Gomorrah. God again saw that man was sinful and reacted in anger. In Genesis 19:24–25 we read, "Then the LORD rained down burning sulfur on Sodom and Gomorrah—from the LORD out of the heavens. Thus He overthrew those cities and the entire plain, including all those living in the cities—and also the vegetation in the land."

Here are three vivid examples of God being angry and punishing people. Three very strong stories showing a God of wrath, a God whom you don't want to get on the bad side of.

In Acts chapter five, verses 3–11, we read again of God's punishment in the story of Ananias and Saphiriah. It reads, "Now a man named Ananias, together with his wife Sapphira, also sold a piece of property. With his wife's full knowledge he kept back part of the money for himself, but brought the rest and put it at the apostles' feet. Then Peter said, 'Ananias, how is it that Satan has so filled your heart that you have lied to the Holy Spirit and have kept for yourself some of the money you received for the land? Didn't it belong to you before it was sold? And after it was sold, wasn't the money at your disposal? What made you think of doing such a thing? You have not lied to men but to God.'"

"When Ananias heard this, he fell down and died. And great fear seized all who heard what had happened. Then the young men came forward, wrapped up his body, and carried him out and buried him. About three hours later his wife came in, not knowing what had happened. Peter asked her, 'Tell me, is this the price you and Ananias got for the land?' 'Yes,' she said, 'that is the price.' Peter said to her, 'How could you agree to test the Spirit of the Lord? Look! The feet of the men who buried your husband are at the door, and they will carry you out also.' At that moment she fell down at his feet and died. Then the young men came in and, finding her dead, carried her out and buried her beside her husband. Great fear seized the whole church and all who heard about these events."

Remember the verse we read about the merciful God in Exodus when He was speaking to Moses? That is the same God that used Pharaoh for His purpose and let him die apart from God.

In Romans 9:14–15 Paul quoting from the chapter in exodus says, "What then shall we say? Is God unjust? Not at all! For He says to Moses, 'I will have mercy on whom I have mercy, and I will have compassion on whom I have compassion.'"

Paul goes on to say, "It does not, therefore, depend on man's desire or effort, but on God's mercy. For the Scripture says to Pharaoh: 'I raised you up for this very purpose, that I might display my power in you and that my name might be proclaimed in all the earth.' Therefore God has mercy on whom He wants to have mercy, and He hardens whom He wants to harden."

God raised Pharaoh up so that God could display His mighty power in bringing Pharaoh down through Moses and the Israelite nation. This clearly demonstrates that there is a side to God that, although perfectly and holy, includes a righteous wrath and vengeance.

Finally, God has created a terrible place for those that don't know Him. In Mark 9:42–49, we get a pretty good picture of this place. It reads, "And if anyone causes one of these little ones who believe in me to sin, it would be better for him to be thrown into the sea with a large millstone tied around his neck. If your hand causes you to sin, cut it off. It is better for you to enter life maimed than with two hands to go into hell, where the fire never goes out. And if your foot causes you to sin, cut it off. It is better for you to enter life crippled than to have two feet and be thrown into hell. And if your eye causes you to sin, pluck it out. It is better for you to enter the kingdom of God with one eye than to have two eyes and be thrown into hell, where `the worm does not die, and the fire is not quenched.' Everyone will be salted with fire."

In the Parable of the Rich Man and Lazarus we can see God's wrath. God tells us this story in Luke 16: 20–31. "There was a rich man who was dressed in purple and fine linen and lived in luxury every day. At his gate was laid a beggar named Lazarus, covered with sores and longing to eat what fell from the rich man's table. Even the dogs came and licked his sores. The time came when the beggar died and the angels carried him to Abraham's side. The rich man also died and was buried. In hell, where he was in torment, he looked up and saw Abraham far away, with Lazarus by his side. So he called to him, `Father Abraham, have pity on me and send Lazarus to dip the tip of his finger in water and cool my tongue, because I am in agony in this fire.' But Abraham replied, `Son, remember that in your lifetime you received your good things, while

Lazarus received bad things, but now he is comforted here and you are in agony. And besides all this, between us and you a great chasm has been fixed, so that those who want to go from here to you cannot, nor can anyone cross over from there to us.' He answered, `Then I beg you, father, send Lazarus to my father's house, for I have five brothers. Let him warn them, so that they will not also come to this place of torment.' Abraham replied, `They have Moses and the Prophets; let them listen to them.' `No, father Abraham,' he said, `but if someone from the dead goes to them, they will repent.' He said to him, `If they do not listen to Moses and the Prophets, they will not be convinced even if someone rises from the dead.'"

God is definitely a god of wrath. He doesn't give second chances. The rich man just wanted to warn his brothers, and God said no. This is the God that Scripture portrays.

Here comes our problem. How can we understand a God that is so good and loving, and yet seemingly vengeful? How can we learn from a God who is has taught us so much about love, and shown us so much of His wrath? How can we believe in a God who sends His only Son to save sinful people, and destroys the world, Sodom and Gomorrah, and drives Adam and Eve from their home? How can we love a God that gives us examples of His Love, and yet takes Ananias and Saphriah's life because of a little white lie? How can we comprehend a God that is loving enough to create Heaven, and vengeful enough to create Hell? How can we trust a God who has extended to us mercy through Christ Jesus, and has condemned all that do not obey Him?

That's the balance that we need to strike.

I believe that there are three things that we need to do, no that we have an obligation to do if we are to have a right relationship with God. A relationship that balances both sides of the coin so that we can see the whole thing. The God that is merciful and loving to those that do what He asks, and wrathful to those that are disobedient to Him.

First of all, we need to know God. There is an expression that says, "First impressions last forever." That is entirely true if that is the only impression that we see. In John 17:25–26, Jesus is praying and He says, "Righteous Father, though the world does not know you, I know you, and they know that you have sent me. I have made you known to them, and will continue to make you known in order that the love you have for me may be in them and that I myself may be in them."

The only way to truly know God is to know Christ. And there is only one way to come to know Christ. First John 2:3–5 says it all. It reads, "We know that we have come to know Him if we obey his commands. The man who says, 'I know Him,' but does not do what He commands is a liar and the truth is not in him. But if anyone obeys His word, God's love is truly made complete in him. This is how we know we are in Him: Whoever claims to live in Him must walk as Jesus did." The only way to know how Jesus lived is to study God's great biography, His Word, the Bible.

How do we have confidence that we know God? It's because we follow His commandments. And the only way we can get to know what His commandments are is through study of His Word. Without truly understanding and studying the Word of God, you can never truly have a relationship with God because you will never be able to strike the balance of understanding. If you don't spend time learning about God, you can never know Him. You can't learn everything God wants you to know about Him from having a "religious experience" at a river side in the mountains. You can not learn all about Him by having a televangelist pray for you. You can not know all about God because you listened to a preacher. You need to study and work at the relationship. Otherwise, you'll never really see both sides of the coin.

Secondly, we need to Love God. Just as God is a God of love, He expects us to be a people of Love. He expects us to Love Him with all of our heart, soul, mind, and strength (Luke 10).

It's important to know what it means to love God. John 14:15 tells us, "'If you love me, you will obey what I command. And I will ask the Father, and He will give you another Counselor to be with you for-ever—the Spirit of truth. The world cannot accept Him, because it neither sees him nor knows Him. But you know Him, for He lives with you and will be in you. I will not leave you as orphans; I will come to you. Before long, the world will not see me anymore, but you will see me. Because I live, you also will live. On that day you will realize that I am in my Father, and you are in me, and I am in you. Whoever has my commands and obeys them, he is the one who loves me. He who loves me will be loved by my Father, and I too will love him and show myself to him.' Then Judas (not Judas Iscariot) said, 'But, Lord, why do you intend to show yourself to us and not to the world?' Jesus replied, 'If anyone loves me, he will obey my teaching. My Father will love him, and we will come to him and make our home with him. He who does not love me will not obey my teaching. These words you hear are not my own; they belong to the Father who sent me.'" So loving God means following His commandments.

John writes again in First John 4:7–21, "Dear friends, let us love one another, for love comes from God. Everyone who loves has been born of God and knows God. Whoever does not love does not know God, because God is love. This is how God showed his love among us: He sent his one and only Son into the world that we might live through him. This is love: not that we loved God, but that He loved us and sent his Son as an atoning sacrifice for our sins. Dear friends, since God so loved us, we also ought to love one another. No one has ever seen God; but if we love one another, God lives in us and His love is made complete in us. We know that we live in Him and He in us, because He has given us of His Spirit. And we have seen and testify that the Father has sent His Son to be the Savior of the world. If anyone acknowledges that Jesus is the Son of God, God lives in him and he in God. And so we know and rely on the love God has for us. God is love. Whoever lives in love lives in God, and God in him. In this way, love is made complete among us so that we will have confidence on the day of judgment, because in this world we are like Him. There is no fear in love. But perfect love drives out fear, because fear has to do with punishment. The one who fears is not made perfect in love. We love because He first loved us. If anyone says, 'I love God,' yet hates his brother, he is a liar. For anyone who does not love his brother, whom he has seen, cannot love God, whom he has not seen. And he has given us this command: Whoever loves God must also love his brother." So loving God means that we need to follow His commandments, and demonstrate the kind of Love that He demonstrated through Christ. Just as Christ said, we must love the Lord our God with all of our heart, mind, and soul, and love our neighbor as ourselves (Matthew 22).

To truly understand God, we need to love Him and follow that example of love that He has shown us, by showing the same love to those around us. We need follow the commandments of God, all of them, as shown in Scripture. Loving God is the foundation of our relationship with Him, just as the foundation of His relationship with us, is His love for us as shown through Christ.

Thirdly, we need to Fear God. Psalm 34:9ff reads, "Fear the LORD, you his saints, for those who fear him lack nothing. The lions may grow weak and hungry, but those who seek the LORD lack no good thing. Come, my children, listen to me; I will teach you the fear of the LORD." We are told in Scripture to fear God.

In Malachi 3:16, it says, "Then those who feared the LORD talked with each other, and the LORD listened and heard." So God pays attention to those that fear Him.

Mary, when she was pregnant with Jesus said to Elizabeth in Luke 1:46–50, "My soul glorifies the Lord and my spirit rejoices in God my Savior, for He has been mindful of the humble state of His servant. From now on all generations will call me blessed, for the Mighty One has done great things for me—holy is His name. His mercy extends to those who fear Him, from generation to generation." God is merciful to those that fear Him.

But what does it mean to fear the Lord? Proverbs 8:13 states, "To fear the LORD is to hate evil." Acts 10:1–2 describes Cornelius. It reads, "At Caesarea there was a man named Cornelius, a centurion in what was known as the Italian Regiment. He and all his family were devout and God-fearing; he gave generously to those in need and prayed to God regularly."

So fearing God, does not mean being afraid of God. It means respecting God's authority over you. That authority is in Christ. Fearing God means respecting the authority of Christ. In Matthew 28:16–18 we read, "Then the eleven disciples went to Galilee, to the mountain where Jesus had told them to go. When they saw him, they worshiped him; but some doubted. Then Jesus came to them and said, 'All authority in heaven and on earth has been given to me.'" You know the rest, but the point is, when Jesus ascended to Heaven, He received ALL POWER AND AUTHORITY, and fearing God means recognizing and humbling ourselves to His authority.

We tend to have a single sided view of God, mainly because we don't open our eyes wide enough to know Him, open our hearts wide enough to love Him, and open our pride wide enough to respect Him. We need to study hard to understand who God is, and what a marvelous gift He has given us in Christ. We need to love each other as God loved us, and keep all of His commandments, proving that we love Him. We need to humble ourselves before His throne and understand that He, and He alone, is omnipotent and omniscient, all powerful and all knowing.

As Paul said in First Corinthians 13:12, "Now we see but a poor reflection as in a mirror; then we shall see face to face."

At some point Christ will return (First Thessalonians 4:16) and we face judgment (Second Corinthians 5:10). There we will have to account for the way we knew or didn't know God.

At some point we will have to account for the way we loved or didn't love God. At some point we will have to account for the way we feared or didn't fear God. At some point we will have to account for our understanding of both sides of the coin. At some point we will have to account for our balance. At some point we will be face-to-face with God. Face-to-face with Christ at the judgment.

I want to hear him say, as in Matthew 25:34, "Come, you who are blessed by my Father; take your inheritance, the kingdom prepared for you since the creation of the world."

Let me share a poem with you.

"Understanding God" by Dana H. Burnell

Sometimes I am afraid of God,
when I read about the flood,
and Sodom and Gomorrah,
and a river full of blood.
I question how a loving God
could let a child die,
and I tremble and I wonder,
as the teardrops fill my eyes.

Sometimes I am at peace with God,
and I marvel at the love,
that would send His only Son to die
from Heaven up above.
I think about forgiveness,
and how much it must have hurt,
to lower Christ from glory,
to live with man upon the dirt.

I always and forever
will be awed by Heaven's plan,
That justice, mercy, and our faith,
is what will save a man.
I always and forever, will be bowed before the
     king,
and the balance of the ages will inspire the saved
     to sing.

If you think of God myopically, or you don't
know God at all, I encourage you to get to know

Him and know Him well. God is awesome and mighty. Be baptized into Christ today and put on the garment that will last eternally.

Chapter 4

One Way : God's Way

*C*hildren have you ever tried to push open a door that reads pull? There is a story about a boy that was in his first year of baseball and he had not hit the ball all year. Then in an important game, he connected with one. It went way into the outfield. He got so excited that he took off running, and as he got to third base, the third base coach screamed at him that he was going the wrong way. We need to make sure that we are finding the right way to God. Wouldn't it be sad if we found a path that we thought led to God but really didn't and as a result we were out because of it?

Ephesians 4:1–6 tells us, "As a prisoner for the Lord, then, I urge you to live a life worthy of the calling you have received. Be completely humble and gentle; be patient, bearing with one another in love.

Make every effort to keep the unity of the Spirit through the bond of peace. There is one body and one Spirit—just as you were called to one hope when you were called—one Lord, one faith, one baptism; one God and Father of all, who is over all and through all and in all." We are to be united in all things.

For a number of reasons I wanted to write about this topic. It has been a thought that has been on my heart for a long time and now I really feel I need to share it with you.

Let me share a story with you.

A few years ago we lived in the Denver, Colorado metro area. There are two major interstate highways that carve their way through Denver. Interstate 25 runs north and south, and Interstate 70 runs east and west. A good deal of interstate 70 is an elevated highway that runs far enough above ground, and is narrow enough that exiting the freeway is only possible at official exits. One afternoon my family and I were headed west on one of the raised portions of interstate 70, and traffic was moving along at about 60 miles an hour. All of a sudden a car was upon us. Driving the wrong way, eastbound in the westbound lanes was an elderly couple in a small car. They were going pretty slowly, but they were hugging the concrete guard rail, and they looked terrified. They were going the wrong way! They were in a very dangerous position. Can we find ourselves in a similar dangerous position where we are going the wrong way in our walk with God?

Do you believe in Satan? Is he real? Is he alive? Is he active in our lives? Scripture plainly shows that Satan is alive and well, powerful and living in our lives today. We need to realize that we have an adversary that will do whatever is within his power to get us to fail, or go the wrong way in our walk with God.

Several Scriptures come to mind to show us that we are engaged in a battle with Satan. Satan is not a coward, he even challenged Christ Himself. In Matthew, 4:1–11 it reads, "Then Jesus was led by the Spirit into the desert to be tempted by the devil. After fasting forty days and forty nights, He was hungry. The tempter came to Him and said, 'If you are the Son of God, tell these stones to become bread.' Jesus answered, 'It is written: "Man does not live on bread alone, but on every word that comes from the mouth of God."' Then the devil took Him to the holy city and had Him stand on the highest point of the temple. 'If you are the Son of God,' he said, 'throw yourself down. For it is written: "He will command his angels concerning you, and they will lift you up in their hands, so that you will not strike your foot against a stone."' Jesus answered him, 'It is also written: "Do not put the Lord your God to the test."' Again, the devil took Him to a very high mountain and showed Him all the kingdoms of the world and their splendor. 'All this I will give you,' he said, 'if you will bow down and worship me.' Jesus said to him, 'Away from me, Satan! For it is written: "Worship the Lord your God, and serve him only."' Then the devil left him, and angels came and attended him."

Second Corinthians 11:14 tells us that, "Satan masquerades as an angel of light." Satan doesn't always look like Satan.

James 4:7 admonishes us to, "Submit yourselves, then, to God. Resist the devil, and he will flee from you."

First Peter 5:8–9 reminds us to, "Be self-controlled and alert. Your enemy the devil prowls around like a roaring lion looking for someone to devour. Resist him, standing firm in the faith, because you know that your brothers throughout the world are undergoing the same kind of sufferings."

Ephesians 6:10–17 tells us to be strong and prepare ourselves for battle with Satan. It reads, "Finally, be strong in the Lord and in his mighty power. Put on the full armor of God so that you can take your stand against the devil's schemes. For our struggle is not against flesh and blood, but against the rulers, against the authorities, against the powers of this dark world and against the spiritual forces of evil in the heavenly realms. Therefore put on the full armor of God, so that when the day of evil comes, you may be able to stand your ground, and after you have done everything, to stand. Stand firm then, with the belt of truth buckled around your waist, with the breastplate of righteousness in place, and with your feet fitted with the readiness that comes from the gospel of peace. In addition to all this, take up the shield of faith, with which you can extinguish all the flaming arrows of the evil one. Take the helmet of salvation and the sword of the Spirit, which is the word of God. And pray in the Spirit on all occasions with all kinds of prayers and requests. With this in mind, be alert and always keep on praying for all the saints."

How many ways does the devil have to try to trick us, or try to lure us away from God? Innumerable! Satan's biggest and strongest tool is to make us believe that there is an easier way, and through small changes to turn the truth of God into a lie, that will condemn us to an eternity away from God.

Have you ever heard the saying, "close only counts in horseshoes and hand grenades?" That is really true. We sometimes see our walk of faith as something that is difficult. It is difficult sometimes, but that doesn't mean we can sidestep the responsibility that it gives.

Let me share another story with you.

Larry was a member of the bomb squad of a major metropolitan city. He had been on the force for 15 years, so he was fairly senior and considered very experienced. He had seen a number of his friends, and a couple of partners killed or hurt in the line of duty, and knew in his heart of hearts that his job was a dangerous one. His wife, Lisa, always kissed him goodbye in the morning and then said a little prayer as he drove away that God would keep him safe.

One day, in the fall of 1987, Larry was called to come to disarm a bomb that was located in the subway. There had been more than one bomb and two others had already exploded, killing several people. This one was inside a subway car far below the streets of the city, and trapped in the wreckage of the other bombs not 10 feet from the ticking bomb, was a 12 year old girl named Abbey. She was very scared and had a large block of cement pinning her legs to the bottom of the subway car.

Larry arrived on the scene like a hero and went to work. He got to the bomb with all of his gear, and started to examine it. It was a fairly common type of detonator. Larry had defused many of these bombs before. Larry knew that there were two ways to defuse this particular type of bomb, the quick way, cutting two of the three wires that lead from the timer to the detonator, or systematically taking the timer apart and stopping its action. The second way would take about 45 minutes.

Larry looked over and saw Abbey as she cried out in pain and fear. He looked at the time on the timer, it read 57 minutes, plenty of time, thought Larry to defuse this the right way. So he started working. About 10 minutes into the operation, Larry found he was distracted by the girl's cries and decided that he should, for the girl's sake, take the quick way. The problem with this way was that you needed to cut the right two wires and there was no sure way to tell which ones they were. It was a game of chance. But Larry reasoned that he knew enough to figure it out, and that, coupled with luck was what would see him through this.

Larry cut the first wire, the white one. The timer kept ticking, but no explosion. Larry was pleased with himself, he knew that he would soon have the little girl out and the work would be complete. He would be a hero again. Nervously he looked at the remaining two wires, red, and green. He thought it looked like Christmas and smiled. He put his cutters to the red wire and squeezed.

The resulting explosion could be heard many blocks away, as tons of concrete and steel came pouring in on the subway car, crushing it and its two inhabitants instantly.

What was Larry's mistake? He believed that there was an easier way. He thought that he could do it better or faster, or easier, by taking a short cut. He believed the truth, but took what looked like an easier path to the same end. Close only counts in horseshoes and hand grenades.

That is exactly the kind of ploy that Satan uses on us. He tries to show us an easier way to salvation, twisting it just enough to make it seem like it's right, yet wrong enough to cost us our salvation.

There are hundreds of "Christian" denominations in the world, all founded on good principals, by good people, in an effort to save souls. There are hundreds of Christian denominations teaching mostly truth, but enough of a lie to condemn people to an eternity apart from God. That is the ploy of Satan. It's his easiest tool, because he leaves people feeling they are right and never knowing the difference. Scripture tells us there is one way, not an alternate way, or an easier way, or a wrong way, but Gods' way. One Body, one Spirit, one Hope, one Lord, one Faith, one Baptism, one God and Father. One way, God's way (Ephesians 4:4).

What do those terms mean?

What does it mean to be united in one Body? Ephesians 1, starting in the middle of verse 20 reads, "That power is like the working of his mighty strength, which He exerted in Christ when He raised Him from the dead and seated Him at His right hand in the heavenly realms, far above all rule and authority, power and dominion, and every title that can be given, not only in the present age but also in the one to come. And God placed all things under His feet and appointed Him to be head over everything for the church, which is His body, the fullness of Him who fills everything in every way."

"One body" is Christ's Church. Satan is a very clever being. He paints all sorts of pictures and puts all sorts of ideas in people's heads in order to lure them from the truth. The "Church" is not a building, it is not some denomination, and it is not a group of rules or collection of ideas. The Church, the Body of Christ, is the sum total of those individuals that have obeyed the Gospel, and have entered into a saving relationship with God through Christ Jesus. But, doesn't that leave out a lot of people? Yes, sadly it does, but truth is truth, God's word cannot be changed. Living in an era of "diversity" like we do, we are conditioned by society to be understanding of the differences in people and their beliefs. This includes everything from sexual orientation, to race, to religious differences. I agree that we need to be compassionate, because that is living in the nature of Christ, but we must never back away from the truth of the Gospel, regardless of the outcome of that decision. If you are not a member of the body of Christ, according to the word of God, you're not a member of His Unity. But everyone who has put on the Lord in baptism and has a scripturally saving relationship with God is a member of His body. It is not a matter of whether we attend a church called the "Church of Christ," but whether we are member of Christ's body that counts. That's what it means to be united in one body.

What does it mean to be united in One Spirit? That One Spirit is the Holy Spirit of God, a divine member of the Trinitarian Godhead. Jesus promised us in John 15 that the Holy Spirit would come to all of us. Verses 25–26 read, "All this I have spoken while still with you. But the Counselor, the Holy Spirit, whom the Father will send in my name, will teach you all things and will remind you of everything I have said to you." We also know that we will be filled with this Spirit when we are baptized. Galatians 3:26–28 reads, "You are all sons of God through faith in Christ Jesus, for all of you who were baptized into Christ have clothed yourselves with Christ. There is neither Jew nor Greek, slave nor free, male nor female, for you are all one in Christ Jesus." A very familiar passage is Acts 2:38, when Peter preaching his first sermon at Pentecost and receiving a great response, told those that responded about baptism. He said, "Repent and let each of you be baptized in the name of Jesus Christ for the remission of your sins and you will receive the gift of the Holy Spirit." The Holy Spirit is real, and is alive in every person that has put on the Lord in baptism and has a scripturally saving relationship with Him. That is what it means to be united in one Spirit.

What does it mean to be united in one hope? The world is very keen on the term hope. As a society of people we hope for many things. We hope for wealth and fame and glory and easier times. We hope that we can have love, we hope for excitement, adventure, and sometimes rest. But for the Christian the term hope has a much greater meaning. Hope is what the Christian lives for! In Colossians 1:27, Paul is speaking about the Gentiles and he says, "To them God has chosen to make known among the Gentiles the glorious riches of this mystery, which is Christ in you, the hope of glory." Titus 2:11–14 describes that hope. It reads, "For the grace of God that brings salvation has appeared to all men. It teaches us to say 'No' to ungodliness and worldly passions, and to live self-controlled, upright and godly lives in this present age, while we wait for the blessed hope—the glorious appearing of our great God and Savior, Jesus Christ, who gave himself for us to redeem us from all wickedness and to purify for himself a people that are his very own, eager to do what is good."

It is this hope, this promise of God, this eternity that awaits us and as Christians is our hope. We see beyond today to understand the future that awaits everyone that has put on the Lord in baptism and has this eternal hope of Heaven. That is what it means to be united in one Hope, the Hope of eternity with God in Heaven.

What does it mean to be united in One Lord? There is only one way to Heaven, period. There is only one way to eternity with God, period. That way is through the death, burial, and resurrection of Jesus Christ!! "For God so loved the world that He gave His one and only Son, that whoever believes in Him shall not perish but have eternal life. For God did not send His Son into the world to condemn the world, but to save the world through Him (John 3:16–17)." The only authority, by which we can be saved, is the authority of Jesus Christ.

Acts 10:36 reads, "You know the message God sent to the people of Israel, telling the good news of peace through Jesus Christ, who is Lord of all." Jesus Christ is the one and only Lord. He is Lord of all of us. It doesn't matter if you're a Muslim, a Catholic, a Jew, or an atheist, truth is truth. We can't change the truth by having a different set of beliefs. We are all united in one Lord, Jesus Christ. Romans 10:12 says "For there is no difference between Jew and Gentile—the same Lord is Lord of all and richly blesses all who call on him, for, 'Everyone who calls on the name of the Lord will be saved.'" This Jesus Christ has all authority and all power. He is the Lord of Lords, and the King of Kings. Matthew 28:18–20 reads, "Then Jesus came to them and said, 'All authority in heaven and on earth has been given to me. Therefore go and make disciples of all nations, baptizing them in the name of the Father and of the Son and of the Holy Spirit, and teaching them to obey everything I have commanded you. And surely I am with you always, to the very end of the age.'" That's what it means to be united in one Lord.

What does it mean to be united in one faith? First we need to answer the question, "What is faith?" Hebrews 11:1 tells us "Now faith is being sure of what we hope for and certain of what we do not see." Faith for the Christian is belief in the promise of God, the Gospel of Christ, and the eternity that awaits us. Galatians 3:26–28 says, "You are all sons of God through faith in Christ Jesus, for all of you who were baptized into Christ have clothed yourselves with Christ." We get this faith by repeated study and communion with God. We need to hear the message, and study the Gospel and really come to a sound relationship with God through Christ. Romans 10:17 says it all. It reads, "Consequently, faith comes from hearing the message, and the message is heard through the word of Christ."

We cannot stop there. We need to then use that faith to change the world around us. We need to portray that faith and that relationship with God to the world around us. They have to see Christ in what we do and who we are. James 2:26 tells us that "As the body without the spirit is dead, so faith without deeds is dead." We need to encourage one another to do the same. We need to meet and study God's word together. We need to meet and fellowship together. We need to come together for worship. For through these things, we are strengthened and truly are united in one faith, the Gospel of Christ.

What does it mean to be united in One Baptism? Many different denominations have taught different things about baptism. There are many interpretations of the method of baptism. Some teach that you should be sprinkled with a little holy water. Some teach that you should be dipped into a little bit of water. There are also many different man made reasons for being baptized. Some denominations teach that you need to be baptized in order to become a member of the local congregation. Others teach that you need to be baptized as a symbol of your faith. No matter what we do, if we do not do it according to what God says, it's meaningless. John 3:3–5 reads, "In reply Jesus declared, 'I tell you the truth, no one can see the kingdom of God unless he is born again.' 'How can a man be born when he is old?' Nicodemus asked. 'Surely he cannot enter a second time into his mother's womb to be born!' Jesus answered, 'I tell you the truth, no one can enter the kingdom of God unless he is born of water and the Spirit.'" Here Jesus is speaking to Nicodemus and clearly explains that baptism by water and Spirit is the only way to God. We need to experience that new birth that comes through baptism into Christ.

In Matthew 3:11 we see the New Testament's first discussion of baptism. Here we read about John the Baptist baptizing people. He says, "I baptize you with water for repentance. But after me will come one who is more powerful than I, whose sandals I am not fit to carry. He will baptize you with the Holy Spirit and with fire." Clearly John says that what he is doing is good, but there is something better coming. These people were being baptized for repentance.

In Acts 19:1–5 we read of some of these people again. It reads, "While Apollos was at Corinth; Paul took the road through the interior and arrived at Ephesus. There he found some disciples and asked them, 'Did you receive the Holy Spirit when you believed?' They answered, 'No, we have not even heard that there is a Holy Spirit.' So Paul asked, 'Then what baptism did you receive?' 'John's baptism,' they replied. Paul said, 'John's baptism was a baptism of repentance.' He told the people to 'believe in the one coming after him, that is, in Jesus.' On hearing this, they were baptized into the name of the Lord Jesus!"

We can clearly see that there is a correct reason to be baptized and that being baptized for the wrong reason means that they were never truly baptized.

But what then is baptism for? In Jesus great commission in Mark 16:15–16, "He said to them, 'Go into all the world and preach the good news to all creation. Whoever believes and is baptized will be saved, but whoever does not believe will be condemned.'" So we can obviously see that one purpose of baptism is salvation. We read in Acts 2:38, at Peters first sermon when the people were asking how they should be saved, Peter replied, "Repent and be baptized, every one of you, in the name of Jesus Christ for the forgiveness of your sins. And you will receive the gift of the Holy Spirit." So the faithful obedience in baptism means that you receive salvation, your sins are forgiven and the Holy Sprit that we spoke of earlier will indwell you to guide and strengthen you in your walk with Christ.

That's fine, for the purpose, but what about the form? Scripture never ever speaks of being dipped or sprinkled. We can see one of the clearest examples of baptism and its form in the New Testament is found in the verses we examined in the earlier part of this book, Acts 8:26–39. It reads, "Now an angel of the Lord said to Philip, 'Go south to the road—the desert road—that goes down from Jerusalem to Gaza.' So he started out, and on his way he met an Ethiopian eunuch, an important official in charge of all the treasury of Candace, queen of the Ethiopians. This man had gone to Jerusalem to worship and on his way home was sitting in his chariot reading the book of Isaiah the prophet. The Spirit told Philip, 'Go to that chariot and stay near it.' Then

Philip ran up to the chariot and heard the man reading Isaiah the prophet. 'Do you understand what you are reading?' Philip asked. 'How can I,' he said, 'unless someone explains it to me?' So he invited Philip to come up and sit with him. The eunuch was reading this passage of Scripture: 'He was led like a sheep to the slaughter and as a lamb before the Shearer is silent, so He did not open his mouth. In His humiliation He was deprived of justice. Who can speak of His descendants? For His life was taken from the earth.'"

"The eunuch asked Philip, 'Tell me, please, who is the prophet talking about, himself or someone else?' Then Philip began with that very passage of Scripture and told him the good news about Jesus. As they traveled along the road, they came to some water and the eunuch said, 'Look, here is water. Why shouldn't I be baptized?' And he gave orders to stop the chariot. Then both Philip and the eunuch went down into the water and Philip baptized him. When they came up out of the water, the Spirit of the Lord suddenly took Philip away, and the eunuch did not see him again, but went on his way rejoicing."

It did not say that they the eunuch was sprinkled, or that he was dipped, but that he went down into the water. Submersion in water is the only vision of baptism ever portrayed in Scripture. Only those who have been baptized in the correct form, and for the correct purpose, with true belief, are scripturally saved and will get to share in eternity with God. That is what it means to be united in one baptism.

What does it mean to be united in One God and Father? There are many many Scriptures that speak of the idea that there is only one God. We take that fact for granted as Christians, but there are many other religions that worship other gods still today. First Timothy, 2:5 tells us that there is one God and one mediator between God and men, the man Christ Jesus. But as far back as the Ten Commandments, we can see that God said we should worship Him only, not other graven images, or other gods of any kind. First Corinthians 8:4–6 shows us that other god's exist. It reads, "So then, about eating food sacrificed to idols: We know that an idol is nothing at all in the world and that there is no god but one. For even if there are so-called gods, whether in heaven or on earth (as indeed there are many 'gods' and many 'lords'), yet for us there is but one God, the Father, from whom all things came and for whom we live; and there is but one Lord, Jesus Christ, through whom all things came and through whom we live."

Herein lies the problem. It's not that we don't believe in God, but that we do not make Him our God. There is one authority in our lives, Jehovah God. When we put other things ahead of Him in our lives we create for ourselves false gods. We submit to authorities other than God. We have other things that we put first in our lives. Matthew 6:24 tells us, "No one can serve two masters. Either he will hate the one and love the other, or he will be devoted to the one and despise the other. You cannot serve both God and money."

Money is just an example; there are many things we make out to be our God, possessions, careers, hobbies, sometimes people. Whenever we put something ahead of our relationship with God, it has become our God.

We need to be united in One God and Father. That means that we need to be united in putting God first in our lives. That has to be our first and strongest commonality and bond. We can be united in other things, but together we are indebted to strengthen each other in this bond first and foremost. Only those that are Scripturally saved, and keep as their only god, the God of Scripture, the God of Heaven and earth, the one and only God and Father of our Lord Jesus Christ, are assured of spending eternity in Heaven with Him.

As we have seen, there are many points to the unity God calls us to. We have also noted that there is crafty being called Satan. He is alive and well and willing to make us change our minds or take the easy way in many cases. I encourage you, as Paul says in Second Timothy 4:7, to "fight the good fight, finish the race, keep the Faith." If you doubt, look in God's Word. That is our strongest weapon against Satan. Because no matter how he tries to deceive or confuse us, if we are strong in our faith, and have a solid knowledge of the Word through study, our foundation will prevail against him.

Let me share a poem with you.

"Many Paths" by Dana H. Burnell

There are many paths we walk through life, and
    many roads to wander.
There are many battles, many strife's, and many
    times to ponder.
As we look we need to find the road, that brings
    eternal pleasure.
The one that takes the Christian home, to our
    eternal treasure.

But be on guard for Satan roams, and knows our
    every sin.
He turns the path that leads to home, and by
    that ploy he'll win.
So we must memorize the path, the valleys and
    the trees.
We must understand the wind, and know by
    name the breeze.

For only if that path is worn, emblazoned in our
    heart,
will we be sure to find our way, when the storms
    of life do start.

And when Satan hides the way to grace, and the
    storms a dark abode,
it is our knowledge of Gods word that keeps us
    on God's road.

Seek, and you will find the one and only way to
the Father, through the Son.

If you have the desire to be with the Lord, I en-
courage you to be baptized into His name today.

LIVING LIKE YOU'RE SAVED

Many times good meaning people work with their loved ones to lead them to Christ, and they consider baptism the victory. Baptism is not the victory it's the indoctrination. It's the point at which Satan begins to take an interest. It's the point at which most people fall away from a budding relationship with God. Luke recorded Christ's teaching on the parable of the seeds. Chapter eight, verses 4–8 tell us, "While a large crowd was gathering and people were coming to Jesus from town after town, He told this parable: 'A farmer went out to sow his seed. As he was scattering the seed, some fell along the path; it was trampled on, and the birds of the air ate it up. Some fell on rock, and when it came up, the plants withered because they had no moisture. Other seed fell among thorns, which grew up with it and choked the plants. Still other seed fell on good soil. It came up and yielded a crop, a hundred times more than was sown.'"

It's just like that with our loved ones that turn to God. Either we forget them and their zeal never grows any roots, or Satan grabs them and they never have a chance to grow, or we neglect them and they fall away, or we nourish and care for them, teach them and love them, and guide them to Christian maturity.

This section is about understanding more than the basics. It's about equipping the Christian with the knowledge and understanding to go the battle with Satan. It's about giving them the power to run the race to the finish line. It's about understanding how to deal with the denominationalism that exists and seeing the Truth of the Way, that the only way to the Father is through the Son. It's about having passion in their relationship with God, understanding Christian character, and using worship as a conduit for praising and drawing nearer to God. Finally, it's about keeping your faith alive and active.

Baptism is more than getting wet. It's a commitment to a new life. Without giving the new born the tools to succeed in their new life, baptism is nothing more than shining Satan's spotlight on a babe and ringing the dinner bell.

Chapter 5

Christian Passion

Let me share a story with you.

If your married, do you remember when you were dating your future spouse? I know for me it was a mixture of euphoria and anxiety. Kathryn was studying the Bible with me. One of the conditions of our dating was that I had to study and go to Church. God sent me the total package there. His teaching, His grace, and the most beautiful messenger Heaven could imagine.

At one point I must have been going on and on to my folks about Kathryn. I don't remember it like this but my parents say that I was spouting "Kathryn this, and Kathryn that, and did you know that Kathryn . . . ." Finally my dad had had enough and he blurted out, "You know, she's got her faults just like anybody else." I was livid and ready to defend her. I was passionate about this girl, and this relationship.

A friend of mine, Jerry, is a great computer scientist. Jerry can do anything he wants with computers. He is literally a genius. His vocation and his avocation have melded into a single focused way of life. Jerry strives to be the very best in his field. He works a ton of hours, typically in the 120 hour a week range. Jerry is constantly studying, reading, and experimenting, and consequently, he is extremely skilled at what he does. Jerry became one of the tops in his company not because he had an idea or a dream. He may have had those. He didn't get to the top because of some chance accident. Jerry worked, and strove, and studied, and toiled to be the best because he was passionate about computer science.

How many of you consider yourselves to be passionate people? Webster's defines passion as: intense emotion such as anger, rage, ardent love, zeal, enthusiasm.

There are lots of examples of famous passionate people.

Oksana Baiul

Oksana was born in 1977. A Ukrainian, Oksana's parents separated when she was 2 years old. Her grandfather gave her her first pair of skates when she was just four. When Oksana put the skates on her feet, she couldn't be stopped. Within three years she began skating in local competitions.

Oksana's mother died of cancer when Oksana was thirteen. Victor Petrenko, Oksana's friend and fellow skater, introduced Oksana to his coach. In 1993, Oksana, a 15 year old girl who had never even competed in a junior competition won the World Championship. In 1994, at the age of 16, she captured the world with her winning performance in the Lillehammer, Norway Olympics, winning the Gold Medal.

Oksana didn't start skating in competitions at the age of five because she dreamed about skating. She didn't win the world championship and Olympic gold at 16 because she dreamed about skating. She won because she acted on that dream. Oksana was passionate about figure skating.

Marion Michael Morrison

Marion Michael Morrison was born in 1907 in Winterset Iowa. When he was six his family moved to California. He grew up as a normal boy with many interests. He was a paperboy, football player, president of the school Latin society and head of his senior class. Michael was a straight A student.

After High School, Michael attended the University of Southern California, where he was a football player. It was during this time that he got a summer job in the movie industry. Michael knew he had found his passion, and he never looked back.

Michael stared in many movies that we'll never remember, but many that we will. Some of his better known films were; "The Fighting Seabees", "The Sands of Iwo Jima", "Chism", "True Grit", "Rooster Cogburn", and the "Shootist".

John Wayne, the Duke will always be remembered as that tall in the saddle, bigger than life, standard of American justice. At 6' 4" he'll be remembered as a patriot, tough as nails, and one of America's greatest action hero's.

John Wayne didn't get to the top of his industry and become an icon because he dreamed of acting. He got there because he worked hard and acted upon his dream. John Wayne was passionate about acting.

John Belushi

John was born in 1949 in Chicago. In high school he excelled at football and was a member of the band. Acting was his first love. In college he acted in many plays and participated in Summer Stock. Belushi and several friends auditioned for Chicago's Second City comedy troupe. Belushi was the only one selected. John became the youngest-ever performer to appear in Second City's "Mainstage" productions.

In 1973, John was hired for the off-Broadway National Lampoon's Lemmings. This was an open door. He participated in future National Lampoon projects. In 1975, John Belushi got his big break as he was cast in NBC's new satirical revue program Saturday Night Live. From there he stared in National Lampoons Animal House, and is probably best known for his character as one of the Blues Brothers.

John Belushi was at the top of his game. He had fame and fortune. But John didn't get to the top because he had a dream. He got to the top because he acted on that dream and worked hard at his craft. John Belushi was passionate about acting and comedy.

Passion is a great motivator. It can be outstanding in terms of achievements and works. Passion is that got to have it, got to get it, can't sleep without it, pit of the stomach, unbridled, intense emotion that can spur mankind on to do wonderful things.

But passion without God only belongs to the world. It can be terrific and horrific at the same time. Passion over one idea or concept can cloud your vision and cause you to neglect other important things. Our priorities must always be kept in order. God and family must always rank first and second, in that order.

Jerry

My friend Jerry, the computer genius, lost this balance. He experienced two lost marriages and became more of a workaholic. His children grew up in another state. His second wife became an alcoholic and has been in and out of treatment for years. Finally Jerry became addicted to cocaine. This all happened because he lost his balance and fell victim to a passion that belonged to the world.

Oksana

In 1996, two years after winning Olympic Gold, and at the age of 18, Oksana Baiul, under the influence of alcohol crashed her lime Green Mercedes in a high speed accident. She had fallen victim to a passion that belonged to the world.

John Wayne

John Wayne died on June 11th 1979 from lung cancer. For all his passion, he couldn't kick his smoking habit. All the passion in the world couldn't even save an American hero. The Duke fell victim to a passion that belonged to the world.

John Belushi

On March 5th, 1982, after living every aspect of life to excess, John Belushi died of a cocaine and heroine overdose. Even a comic genius can't get the last laugh when he becomes a victim of a passion that belongs to the world.

Passion needs something to be passionate about. It needs something to throw its arms about, something to hold dear, something to love. With a passion that belongs to the world the object of that passion can be anything.

Worldly passion is putting things before God. Lots of us get into a rut of being ruled by our worldly passions, especially money and work. Jesus warned us of this in Matthew 6:24. It reads, "No one can serve two masters. Either he will hate the one and love the other, or he will be devoted to the one and despise the other. You cannot serve both God and Money."

Jesus didn't say that money was bad. Paul later said that "the love of money is a root of all kinds of evil. Some people, eager for money, have wandered from the faith and pierced themselves with many grief's (First Timothy 6:10)." That word "eager", really means passionate.

Here's a test: Have you ever missed an important event, a family or church event because of a football or baseball game? How about shopping? Computer games? A concert? Boyfriends or girlfriends? Golf? Fishing or hunting? Soccer games? Other hobbies? Work?

How about this one: Do you ever give God less that you give other things? Where do you spend your time? Your money? What has control of your heart?

Whenever you make a decision to place one activity or thing ahead of another, that tells you which of the two you're more passionate about. We can live lives that are out of balance and put worldly passion ahead of Godly passion. Are you passionate like that?

Whenever we feel out of balance in our lives, we need to look at what our passions are. We need to look at who or what we are devoting our hearts to. When we feel out of balance it's typically because we have a passion or passions borne of the world, and perhaps we're fooling ourselves into believing our Godly passions are greater than they truly are.

What, then is Godly passion? Godly passion is that same kind of pit of the stomach, got to do it, got to have it, got to be it, unbridled, all controlling, intense, got to be the best, desire as worldly passion. The difference is that the object of that desire, that passion, is God. It's when the actions spurred by that passion are founded in our love for God. With a Godly passion your first thoughts are of your love for God. Your calendar is filled first with activities that glorify God. The first check you write on payday is for the Lord. Worship is a time that takes second place to nothing else. Your neighbor's soul is of utmost importance and you'll do all that you can do to win them to Christ. Are you passionate like that?

Godly passion means having a zeal for God that cannot be quenched. It means fully realizing, by the actions of our lives, the two greatest commandments as found in Matthew 33:37. They are to love the Lord your God with all your heart and with all your soul and with all your mind. And to love your neighbor as yourself. Godly passion means that these two commandments are the foundation of everything we do.

If we had passion for God the way that commandment reads, we couldn't keep quiet about the grace we've received from God through Christ. If we had passion for our neighbor the way that commandment reads, we would do anything to see them saved. If we had a passion for God the way that commandment reads, we'd have trouble focusing on anything but God. Our love for Him would rule our every action. Our Love for Him would be the foundation of every thought. Our Love for Him would spur us on to the greatest love for each other that you could ever imagine. Are you passionate like that?

We can see through history that there have been passionate men and women. There have been many men and women passionate enough for God to be moved to action. Let's look at some examples of people that were passionate for God, people that had Godly passion.

Moses

Moses was born the son of an Israelite woman in a time when it was a dangerous thing to be an Israelite baby boy. His mother tried to hide him in the reeds of the Nile River and he was found by Pharaoh's daughter. He was raised by Pharaohs daughter and had his own mother as a nanny. He lived for 40 years in the lap of luxury. His mother taught him about his heritage and after seeing an Egyptian murder a Hebrew, he became enraged. He killed the Egyptian (Exodus 2).

Then Moses fled and lived as a shepherd for 40 years. That's when God stepped in. In the form of a burning bush, God appeared to Moses. God instructed Moses and Moses did as he was instructed (Exodus 3). Moses worked to convince Pharaoh, through many plagues, to set free the Hebrew nation. Then Moses led this vast nation, over a million in number, through the desert for 40 years. The people became hard hearted and disobedient to God, over and over again. But, Moses kept on doing God's will and leading them (Exodus 32, Numbers 12, Leviticus 10, Numbers 16).

How do you suppose an 80 year old shepherd summoned the courage to make demands of one of the most powerful men of that time, Pharaoh of Egypt? How do you suppose an 80 year old shepherd summoned the conviction to lead a nation of a million plus, through rebellion and grace, through the desert for 40 years?

Moses had Godly passion. Moses was passionate for God. His love and passion caused him to take action. That action led the Israelite people to the Promised Land.

Solomon

Solomon was the King of Israel, the son of David, and the mightiest king that had ever lived. He was a very reverent man, humble before God. Solomon was a man who was very passionate for God.

Solomon was given the opportunity to ask God for whatever he wished. In First Kings 3:5–15 we see, "At Gibeon the LORD appeared to Solomon during the night in a dream, and God said, 'Ask for whatever you want me to give you.' Solomon answered, 'You have shown great kindness to your servant, my father David, because he was faithful to you and righteous and upright in heart. You have continued this great kindness to him and have given him a son to sit on his throne this very day. Now, O LORD my God, you have made your servant king in place of my father David. But I am only a little child and do not know how to carry out my duties. Your servant is here among the people you have chosen, a great people, too numerous to count or number. So give your servant a discerning heart to govern your people and to distinguish between right and wrong. For who is able to govern this great people of yours?' The Lord was pleased that Solomon had asked for this. So God said to him, 'Since you have asked for this and not for long life or wealth for yourself, nor have asked for the death of your enemies but for discernment in administering justice, I will do what you have asked. I will give you a wise and discerning heart, so that there will never have been anyone like you, nor will there ever be. Moreover, I will give you what you have not asked for—both riches and honor—so that in your lifetime you will have no equal among kings. And if you walk in my ways and obey my statutes and commands as David your father did, I will give you a long life.'"

Solomon became a king as a child. Some accounts say that he was only 12–15 years of age. He also had great and numerous writings. He wrote two of the Psalms, Proverbs, Ecclesiastes, and the Song of Solomon. What inspired such a young man to have what it takes to be King? What inspired such a great young man, when given the chance to ask anything of God, to simply ask for wisdom? What inspired such a man to write some of the greatest books of the Old Testament? Solomon was passionate for

God. Not only did he love God, but he acted upon that love to live a life pleasing before God.

Paul

Paul was born a Pharisee. He was of one of the most learned sect of the Jewish faith, a Roman citizen, educated in some of the best Jewish schools that existed. Paul was a staunch supporter of God. This heart for God led him to persecute the Christians, even killing some.

God changed Paul, who was called Saul. He was stopped on the road to Damascus by the Lord. Acts 9:1–20 reads, "Meanwhile, Saul was still breathing out murderous threats against the Lord's disciples. He went to the high priest and asked him for letters to the synagogues in Damascus, so that if he found any there who belonged to the Way, whether men or women, he might take them as prisoners to Jerusalem. As he neared Damascus on his journey, suddenly a light from heaven flashed around him. He fell to the ground and heard a voice say to him, 'Saul, Saul, why do you persecute me?' 'Who are you, Lord?' Saul asked. 'I am Jesus, whom you are persecuting,' He replied. 'Now get up and go into the city, and you will be told what you must do.' The men traveling with Saul stood there speechless; they heard the sound but did not see anyone. Saul got up from the ground, but when he opened his eyes he could see nothing. So they led him by the hand into Damascus. For three days he was blind, and did not eat or drink anything. In Damascus there was a disciple named Ananias. The Lord called to him in a vision, 'Ananias!' 'Yes, Lord,' he answered. The Lord told him, 'Go to the house of Judas on Straight Street and ask for a man from Tarsus named Saul, for he is praying. In a vision he has seen a man named Ananias come and place his hands on him to restore his sight.' 'Lord,' Ananias answered, 'I have heard many reports about this man and all the harm he has done to your saints in Jerusalem. And he has come here with authority from the chief priests to arrest all who call on your name.' But the Lord said to Ananias, 'Go! This man is my chosen instrument to carry my name before the Gentiles and their kings and before the people of Israel. I will show him how much he must suffer for my name.' Then Ananias went to the house and entered it. Placing his hands on Saul, he said, 'Brother Saul, the Lord—Jesus, who appeared to you on the road as you were coming here—has sent me so that you may see again and be filled with the Holy Spirit.' Immediately, something like scales fell from Saul's eyes, and he could see again. He got up and was baptized, and after taking some food, he regained his strength. Saul spent several days with the disciples in Damascus. At once he began to preach in the synagogues that Jesus is the Son of God."

Paul spent the rest of his life preaching the good news about Jesus. He was one of the most highly persecuted Apostles. He writes about this in Second Corinthians 1:24–28. It reads, "Are they servants of Christ? (I am out of my mind to talk like this.) I am more. I have worked much harder, been in prison more frequently, been flogged more severely, and been exposed to death again and again. Five times I received from the Jews the forty lashes minus one. Three times I was beaten with rods, once I was stoned, three times I was shipwrecked, I spent a night and a day in the open sea, I have been constantly on the move. I have been in danger from rivers, in danger from bandits, in danger from my own countrymen, in danger from Gentiles; in danger in the city, in danger in the country, in danger at sea; and in danger from false brothers. I have labored and toiled and have often gone without sleep; I have known hunger and thirst and have often gone without food; I have been cold and naked. Besides everything else, I face daily the pressure of my concern for all the churches."

Towards the end of his life, Paul recounts his faithful obedience to God. In Second Timothy 4:6–8 we see, "For I am already being poured out like a drink offering, and the time has come for my departure. I have fought the good fight, I have finished the race, I have kept the faith. Now there is in store for me the crown of righteousness, which the Lord, the righteous Judge, will award to me on that day—and not only to me, but also to all who have longed for his appearing."

The uncanny thing about Paul is that he always lived life with a clean conscious. Even when he was persecuting and killing Christians he was a man with a heart for God. Paul lived his whole life in subjection to God.

Paul is the major author of the New Testament, writing at least 13 of those books. What inspired someone like Paul to be such a prolific writer for God? What inspired someone like Paul to live his life fully for God? What inspired someone like Paul to endure all the things he suffered without giving up, and without ever blaming or turning his face from God? Paul was passionate for God. Paul not only loved God, but he acted on that love to make God the center of his life. Paul was passionate for God.

Jesus

Jesus was the one human being that lived most passionately for God. He lived a life without sin, for sin would have drawn Him away from His Father. Jesus lived, loved, healed, prayed, and preached, all for His love of the Father. Jesus was passionate for God.

Jesus was also passionate for mankind. He suffered a flogging, ridicule, scorn, mockery for mans sake. Then He paid the ultimate price and was put to death on a cross. That was an agonizing, painful death. Death, however, was the smaller price. The great price He paid was to take on the sins of all mankind, past, present, and future. He suffered the Fathers abandonment for the first time in all eternity. Jesus was passionate for mankind.

We can dream about being passionate for God all day, but it won't do any good unless like Moses, like Solomon, like Paul, like Jesus, we act on that dream and do something about it.

James says in James 2:17 that, faith by itself, if it is not accompanied by action, is dead. What James is saying is that our faith, our passion for God, is demonstrated by the actions of our lives. We need to make God the center of that faith, and live for Him with unbounded, unbridled passion. That's the meaning of the greatest commandment. That's the fulfillment of the greatest commandment. Remember the greatest commandment? "Love the Lord your God with all your heart and with all your soul and with all your mind (Matthew 22:37)."

With that kind of passion, we can do greater things for our Lord then John Wayne did for the movie industry, then John Belushi did for comedy, then Oksana Baiul did for figure skating. We can have lives led for God, lives where God can use us for mighty things. Like Moses, Solomon, and Paul, we can be God's servants and love Him passionately.

Now, some of you will say to yourselves that you're just not like that. You're just not someone that shows passion. You're objective. You're not bubbly. You're more of a serious type. And you may insist that you're not good at talking to people. You're not outgoing. You're not comfortable talking about Jesus or you don't think you know enough Bible to be effective. None of that matters. A heart truly passionate for God will find a way. A heart truly passionate for God will let Him use our weaknesses to glorify Him. With a passionate love for God we can effect Godly change.

What does that mean, to effect Godly change? It means that through a passionate love for God we can effect Godly change in our lives. Galatians 5:22 shows us what we term the "fruits of the Spirit." These are attributes that we will have in our lives if we are living passionately for God. These include love, joy, peace, patience, kindness, good-ness, faithfulness, gentleness, and self control. Liv-ing a passionate life for God means that we will show more love, feel more peace, have more joy, exhibit more patience, spread more kindness, do more good, live more faithfully, touch hearts more gently, and focus our hearts more earnestly on God. So, with a passionate love for God, we can be bet-ter servants of God and live lives more fulfilling, joyful, and pleasing to God. With a passionate love for God, we can effect Godly change in our lives. But that's not all . . .

Through a passionate love for God, we can ef-fect Godly change in our families. Imagine if we were fully living for God, what that could do to our families. As husband and wife, we could always act out of love, putting our spouses first. We would be terrific examples as parents and tenor all of our parental guidance with a love for God. Scriptures that tell wives to be in subjection to their husbands, and husbands to treat their wives with love and respect would be easy to follow. The Scriptures that tell children to be obedient to their parents would be easy to follow. The things that we teach each other and the stability of our families would be based on God. The divorce and abortion rates would dramatically decline, and families would be stronger. Through a passionate love for God we can effect Godly change in our lives and in our families. But that's not all . . .

Through a passionate love for God we can effect Godly change in our Church congregations. Imagine what it would be like if we always, without fail, looked to God for guidance. We would never argue or split over the trivial things. We would never have feelings of ill will towards a brother or a sister. We would be stronger, drawing strength from each other. We would be better able to evangelize. People would more fully see the difference in us and realize that the difference they see is God. We could inspire more people to follow God, the Church would grow, and the great commission would be fulfilled. With a passionate love for God we can effect Godly change in our lives, in our families, and even in our Churches. But that's not all . . .

With a passionate love for God, we could effect Godly change in our communities. Imagine if all the families that came to your church were passionately committed. The Church would be growing by leaps and bounds. Soon the Church would contain mayors, policemen, businessmen, and council members. We would have God's will working and active in local government. We would have God's will working and active in local industry. We would have God's will working and active throughout our communities. With a passionate love for God, we can effect Godly change in our lives, in our families, in our Churches, and in our communities. But that's not all . . .

With a passionate love for God, we could effect Godly change in our nation. If all of the communities were changing to be founded on a love for God, soon we would have senators, governors, politicians, doctors, and lawyers living committed lives for God. With a passionate love for God we can effect Godly change in our lives, in our families, in our Churches, in our communities, and even in our nation. But that's not all . . .

With a passionate love for God, we can effect Godly change in our world. Imagine if the greatest industrial nation on the planet had its roots and pathways focused on the teachings of God through Christ. Imagine the influence that nation would have on the world. We could be examples of Christian love to the entire world. We could influence Godly change across the globe. With a passionate love for God, we can effect Godly change in our lives, in our families, in our Churches, in our communities, in our country, and even in our world.

It may seem a bit odd to think of the world being influenced and run according to the teachings of God, but God is the creator of the world, so He has the right to set the rules. In the Old Testament (Genesis 3) God dealt directly with people. He gave them personal instruction. At that time His verbal rules were for the entire world. Later God worked through the Priests (Exodus 29) and the instruction was given to the Nation of Israel. Finally, God gave us Jesus (John 3:16). Jesus said, "Go unto all the world and preach the Gospel, that whosoever shall believe and be baptized shall not perish, but shall have everlasting life." (Mark 16:15–16) God wants to use us to effect Godly change in the world.

God has commanded us to fulfill the great commission as found in Matthew 28:18–20 which reads, "Then Jesus came to them and said, 'All authority in heaven and on earth has been given to me. Therefore go and make disciples of all nations, baptizing them in the name of the Father and of the Son and of the Holy Spirit, and teaching them to obey everything I have commanded you. And surely I am with you always, to the very end of the age.'"

Wait a minute, is that talking to us? Yes, this is a circular commandment. The eleven Apostles were told to GO to everyone everywhere, Disciple everyone everywhere to be learners of God, Baptize everyone everywhere to be children of God, Teach everyone everywhere to be submissive to God, and in that submission, everyone everywhere needs to obey all of God's commands, including the command found in this passage. It wasn't a command specially created for the eleven. It was a command specially created for the growth of the Kingdom of God.

God desires and covets our passion. He even commands it. He inspired both Matthew (22:37) and Mark (12:30) to capture that greatest commandment, "You shall love the Lord your God with all your heart, and with all your soul, and with all your mind, and with all your strength."

Not some of our heart, ALL of it.
Not some of our soul, ALL of it.
Not some of our mind, ALL of it.
Not some of our strength, ALL of it.
THIS is passion.

So I ask you today, are you passionate? Is your passion borne of the world, or borne of God? Are you living like you love the Lord your God with every ounce of everything you have?

Do you attend worship because you love God so zealously that you couldn't miss an opportunity to worship Him? Or do you attend because it's one of the three hours a week you've set aside for God? Do the love of God and your passion for Him flow from you so freely that you couldn't hide it if you had too? Or is it a suit that you can put on when you need to look your very best?

God gave us Jesus, and through Him we receive Gods grace. If you understand the enormity of that you understand that nothing else matters. Nothing else matters. All that matters is holding fast to His teachings, running towards the narrow gate, getting up every time we stumble, and bringing everyone we can with us.

There are three places our passion can lead us in our spiritual walk. We can be running to God, with all our zeal, living our passion for Him in such a way that it cannot be unnoticed. We can be rejoicing every day that we can live for Him, and looking forward to the day of His return. The second place that we can be is running away from God. We can be running towards the passions of the world. We can be finding our limited joys and victories in fading memories, not even knowing that our path will never take us where we long to go. We can be running away from the one true source of joy and peace. We can be running away from His grace. A third place we can be is standing still. We can have one foot on each side of the fence, feeling like we are secure and maybe have done enough to win or earn our salvation. We can be waiting to see what the rest of the crowd does, worrying about the gift of grace, and whether or not we are to be the recipients of this gift.

Let me share a poem with you.

"Lord Keep Me in the Race" by Dana H. Burnell

Lord I want to live my life the way that you de-
    sire.
I want to run for you dear Lord and never ever
    tire.
Your glory, holiness, and love inspire and spur
    me on.
I pray I never tire and the entire race I run.

Lord I understand this race I'll fail if run alone.
I need the strength that comes from He who sits
    upon the throne.
So I ask you now my Father, transcend time as
    by your grace,
and keep my feet upon the course, my heart
    within the race.

If your running towards God with unbridled passion, Amen. Go, a reward awaits you. If you're running away from God, stop and turn around. You've never run so far to get away from God. No matter how long, how fast, or how far you've run, God's hand is outstretched right behind you. Turn around and take it. Let Him lead you from the rat race, back to the right race. If you sitting on the fence, remember what Revelation 3:15–16 says, "I know your deeds, that you are neither cold nor hot. I wish you were either one or the other! So, because you are lukewarm—neither hot nor cold—I am about to spit you out of my mouth."

I encourage you to ask your Christian family for prayers. Be strong in the Lord. Run the race with passion. If you need to establish a relationship with God, I encourage you to do so today.

Chapter 6

Christian Character

*W*hat do you think of when you think of the term character? Do you think of someone that is a character, funny, laughable, entertaining. Or do you think of core traits such as honesty, and integrity. This chapter examines Christian character as a basis for our continued walk with God. It explores the kind of character that is exhibited as a reflection of a true Christian heart within.

The world thinks of character in one way. They think of character in terms of Webster's definition. "The qualities that distinguish one person from another. A distinguishing feature or attribute. A structure, function, or attribute determined by a gene or a group of genes. Moral or ethical strength. Reputation."

When I think of character, I think of the foundation of a person. What they are on the inside, not what people think of them, and not what kind of reputation they have developed. Many corrupt politicians have a decent reputation, and present an outward view of moral and ethical excellence. Character is much deeper than that. Character is the strength we have when life is not easy, when it gets tough.

I once heard it said that you can tell what kind of character a man has by the words that come out of his mouth when he smacks his thumb with a hammer. While that's not necessarily true in all cases, it's a pretty good indicator.

Character is an internal trait so basic and fundamental that it carves out the rest of who we are. It is the cornerstone of our personality, and the bedrock of our relationship with other men, and with God. And the truest measure of character is how we deal with adversity.

We all encounter adversity in our lives. We each have our own individual filter through which we see life. That filter is made up of our strengths, our weaknesses, our fears, our skills, our experiences, our faith, and many other factors. But each being individually different, we all see adversity differently as well.

A small child may see a spelling test as a major adversity. A faithful older person may not even see impending death as an adversity. So to define what I mean by adversity is really kind of tough, but it is those things that individually we see as challenges that are difficult to overcome. Adversities are those things that get in the way of our happiness in our relationship with God.

Adversity is a powerful force. First Peter 1:3–7 says, "Praise be to the God and Father of our Lord Jesus Christ! In His great mercy He has given us new birth into a living hope through the resurrection of Jesus Christ from the dead, and into an inheritance that can never perish, spoil or fade—kept in heaven for you, who through faith are shielded by God's power until the coming of the salvation that is ready to be revealed in the last time. In this you greatly rejoice, though now for a little while you may have had to suffer grief in all kinds of trials. These have come so that your faith—of greater worth than gold, which perishes even though refined by fire—may be proved genuine and may result in praise, glory and honor when Jesus Christ is revealed."

There are many examples of overcoming adversity in Scripture. Moses as he dealt with Pharaoh in the book of Exodus, Noah dealing with scorners before the flood in the book of Genesis, Joseph dealing with his brothers and imprisonment in the book of Genesis, and Zacchaeus dealing with his height problems in Luke chapter 19, are all good examples. Paul is the greatest example. In Second Corinthians 6:3–10 he writes, "We put no stumbling block in anyone's path, so that our ministry will not be discredited. Rather, as servants of God we commend ourselves in every way: in great endurance; in troubles, hardships and distresses; in beatings, imprisonments and riots; in hard work, sleepless nights and hunger; in purity, understanding, patience and kindness; in the Holy Spirit and in sincere love; in truthful speech and in the power of God; with weapons of righteousness in the right hand and in the left; through glory and dishonor, bad report and good report; genuine, yet regarded as impostors; known, yet regarded as unknown; dying, and yet we live on; beaten, and yet not killed; sorrowful, yet always rejoicing; poor, yet making many rich; having nothing, and yet possessing everything."

In Romans 5:1–5 Paul writes, "Therefore, since we have been justified through faith, we have peace with God through our Lord Jesus Christ, through whom we have gained access by faith into this grace in which we now stand. And we rejoice in the hope of the glory of God. Not only so, but we also rejoice in our sufferings, because we know that suffering produces perseverance; perseverance, character; and character, hope. And hope does not disappoint us, because God has poured out his love into our hearts by the Holy Spirit, whom He has given us." Paul endured a lot of adversity, but always kept the faith and gave the glory to God. His character shown through.

We see examples of adversity in more modern times that have been overcome.

Look at the story of Abraham Lincoln.

- In 1831 his business failed.
- In 1832 he was defeated in a campaign for the legislature.
- In 1833 he had a second business fail.
- In 1836 he suffered a nervous breakdown.
- In 1838 he was defeated in a campaign for speaker.
- In 1840 he was defeated in a campaign for elector.
- In 1843 he was defeated in a campaign for congress.
- In 1848 he was defeated in a campaign for congress.
- In 1855 he was defeated in a campaign for the senate.
- In 1856 he was defeated in a campaign for vice president.
- In 1858 he was defeated in a campaign for the senate.
- In 1860 he was elected President of the United States.

Martin Luther King is another great example. His home was bombed. He was rebuked. His life was threatened, and eventually he was killed. But his character shone through.

Christopher Reeve is a more recent example. His spinal cord was severed in a horse riding accident in the spring of 1995 leaving him a quadriplegic. Reeves has not given up. Even though he needs a ventilator to breath, he remains active in advocacy, employed as an actor and director, and involved as a husband and father.

Peter is an excellent example from Scripture. In Matthew 26, starting in verse 69, we read, "Now Peter was sitting out in the courtyard, and a servant girl came to him. 'You also were with Jesus of Galilee' she said. But he denied it before them all. 'I don't know what you're talking about,' he said. Then he went out to the gateway, where another girl saw him and said to the people there, 'This fellow was with Jesus of Nazareth.' He denied it again, with an oath: 'I don't know the man!' After a little while, those standing there went up to Peter and said, 'Surely you are one of them, for your accent gives you away.' Then he began to call down curses on himself and he swore to them, 'I don't know the man!' Immediately a rooster crowed. Then Peter remembered the word Jesus had spoken: 'Before the rooster crows, you will disown me three times.' And he went outside and wept bitterly."

Then we see later, that Peter overcame that adversity and became a powerful advocate for Christ. In Acts chapter two, beginning in verse 14 it reads, "Then Peter stood up with the Eleven, raised his voice and addressed the crowd: 'Fellow Jews and all of you who live in Jerusalem, let me explain this to you; listen carefully to what I say. These men are not drunk, as you suppose. It's only nine in the morning! No, this is what was spoken by the prophet Joel: "In the last days, God says, I will pour out my Spirit on all people. Your sons and daughters will prophesy, your young men will see visions, your old men will dream dreams. Even on my servants, both men and women, I will pour out my Spirit in those days, and they will prophesy. I will show wonders in the heaven above and signs on the earth below, blood and fire and billows of smoke. The sun will be turned to darkness and the moon to blood before the coming of the great and glorious day of the Lord. And everyone who calls on the name of the Lord will be saved."'"

Continuing in verse 22 and following it reads, "Men of Israel, listen to this: Jesus of Nazareth was a man accredited by God to you by miracles, wonders and signs, which God did among you through Him, as you yourselves know. This man was handed over to you by God's set purpose and foreknowledge; and you, with the help of wicked men, put Him to death by nailing him to the cross. But God raised Him from the dead, freeing Him from the agony of death, because it was impossible for death to keep its hold on Him. David said about him: 'I saw the Lord always before me. Because He is at my right hand, I will not be shaken. Therefore my heart is glad and my tongue rejoices; my body also will live in hope, because you will not abandon me to the grave, nor will you let your Holy One see decay. You have made known to me the paths of life; you will fill me with joy in your presence.'"

Verse 29 and following goes on to say, "Brothers, I can tell you confidently that the patriarch David died and was buried, and his tomb is here to this day. But he was a prophet and knew that God had promised him on oath that he would place one of his descendants on his throne. Seeing what was ahead, he spoke of the resurrection of the Christ, that He was not abandoned to the grave, nor did His body see decay. God has raised this Jesus to life, and we are all witnesses of the fact. Exalted to the right hand of God, He has received from the Father the promised Holy Spirit and has poured out what you now see and hear. For David did not ascend to heaven, and yet he said, 'The Lord said to my Lord: "Sit at my right hand until I make your enemies a footstool for your feet."' Therefore let all Israel be assured of this: God has made this Jesus, whom you crucified, both Lord and Christ." "When the people heard this, they were cut to the heart and said to Peter and the other apostles, 'Brothers, what shall we do?' Peter replied, 'Repent and be baptized, every one of you, in the name of Jesus Christ for the forgiveness of your sins. And you will receive the gift of the Holy Spirit. The promise is for you and your children and for all who are far off—for all whom the Lord our God will call.' With many other words he warned them; and he pleaded with them, 'Save yourselves from this corrupt generation.' Those who accepted his message were baptized, and about three thousand were added to their number that day." Peter's character shown through.

But there are also times when adversity has not been overcome. We have all heard stories of people that have lost their will to live. People who have given up and succumbed to the worries of the world.

Let me share a story with you.

When I lived in Nebraska, there was a man who was a farmer. He was highly respected in the community. He had worked hard all of his life and had developed a good reputation for himself. And then he discovered gambling. He caught the gambling fever and before long he was in trouble. He tried very hard to "gamble" his way out of trouble, but it only got worse. One day, when he found himself many thousands of dollars in debt and with no visible way out, he drove home, and sitting in his pickup, he pulled out a gun and took his life. He left his family with a ton of debt and left the world in a cowardly fashion. He did, though, just as Abraham Lincoln, or Christopher Reeve, show his character.

In Matthew 26:14–15 it reads, "Then one of the Twelve—the one called Judas Iscariot—went to the chief priests and asked, 'What are you willing to give me if I hand Him over to you?' So they counted out for him thirty silver coins. From then on Judas watched for an opportunity to hand Him over."

Then in verse 47 we read, "While he was still speaking, Judas, one of the Twelve, arrived. With him was a large crowd armed with swords and clubs, sent from the chief priests and the elders of the people. Now the betrayer had arranged a signal with them: 'The one I kiss is the man; arrest him.' Going at once to Jesus, Judas said, 'Greetings, Rabbi!' and kissed him. Jesus replied, 'Friend, do what you came for.'"

Finally in chapter 17, starting in verse three it says, "When Judas, who had betrayed Him, saw that Jesus was condemned, he was seized with remorse and returned the thirty silver coins to the chief priests and the elders. 'I have sinned,' he said, 'for I have betrayed innocent blood.' 'What is that to us?' they replied. 'That's your responsibility.' So Judas threw the money into the temple and left. Then he went away and hanged himself."

Judas was a man of character, poor character. He too was overcome by the adversity of his sin.

So there are a couple of ways that we can deal with adversity and more than one type of character that we can portray. The important thing is to understand the difference.

What is different about the people that are able to overcome adversity, and those that succumb to it? Is it personal strength? Is it a lack of, or a greater understanding? Could it be that they don't see adversity in the same manner? It's really a matter of what that person is on the inside that determines how they will handle the struggles of life. There are four things that make you win over adversity.

The first is vision. People that overcome adversity seem to have a different kind of vision. They see adversity not as something to be battled, but something to be learned from. Napoleon Hill penned the saying "Every adversity carries with it a seed of equivalent or greater benefit." This means that each adversity is a learning experience, a tempering of our wills, and a strengthening of our character (James 1:2–3). Understanding this is the basis for really understanding our relationship with God. God tries us and tests us that we may be perfected in Him. In the example we looked at in Christopher Reeve, we see that he has the vision that because of who he is, and his afflictions, he can do good and raise money for research. In Peter's example, we see that his vision changed and he became an awesome crusader for Christ.

The second is honesty. People that are able to overcome adversity in many ways do so because they are honest about themselves and their situation. Christopher Reeve had to be honest and understand that he was now an invalid and needed help to even breathe. This needed to be there before he could begin to grow again. Admitting that we are weak and in need of help is the basis for character. God says that all have fallen short of His glory. We need to be honest and understand that we don't have to carry the load ourselves. We have a God that is powerful and alive. We are exhorted to come to each other for prayer and for help. We are exhorted to confess our sins and lay our problems before the Church (James 5:16).

The third is humility. We so want to have pride in ourselves. We sometimes see adversity as something to get pity for. We think we are deserving. We hold our own pity-parties and succumb to our own feelings of, "Why Me?" If we are humble, though, we can see that there may be a greater reason for our adversity. We can understand that that we may be used by God for purposes that we don't even comprehend.

Second Corinthians 4:7–12 reads, "But we have this treasure in jars of clay to show that this all-surpassing power is from God and not from us. We are hard pressed on every side, but not crushed; perplexed, but not in despair; persecuted, but not abandoned; struck down, but not destroyed. We always carry around in our body the death of Jesus, so that the life of Jesus may also be revealed in our body. For we who are alive are always being given over to death for Jesus' sake, so that his life may be revealed in our mortal body. So then, death is at work in us, but life is at work in you."

The fourth is bedrock. People who can overcome adversity with character can do so because they have as the bedrock of their lives Jesus Christ. Psalm 22:1–4 tells us, "David sang to the LORD the words of this song when the LORD delivered him from the hand of all his enemies and from the hand of Saul. He said: 'The LORD is my rock, my fortress and my deliverer; my God is my rock, in whom I take refuge, my shield and the horn of my salvation. He is my stronghold, my refuge and my savior—from violent men you save me. I call to the LORD, who is worthy of praise, and I am saved from my enemies.'" Even the Old Testament Israelites had their strength from the Rock of Christ.

In First Corinthians 10:1–4 we read, "For I do not want you to be ignorant of the fact, brothers, that our forefathers were all under the cloud and that they all passed through the sea. They were all baptized into Moses in the cloud and in the sea. They all ate the same spiritual food and drank the same spiritual drink; for they drank from the spiritual rock that accompanied them, and that rock was Christ."

All four of these things are summed up by Paul in Second Corinthians 12:7–10. It says, "To keep me from becoming conceited (humility) because of these surpassingly great revelations, there was given me a thorn in my flesh (honesty), a messenger of Satan, to torment me. Three times I pleaded with the Lord to take it away from me. But He said to me, 'My grace is sufficient for you, for my power is made perfect in weakness.' Therefore I will boast all the more gladly about my weaknesses, so that Christ's power may rest on me (vision). That is why, for Christ's sake (bedrock), I delight in weaknesses, in insults, in hardships, in persecutions, in difficulties. For when I am weak, then I am strong."

The way that we show true character is by taking our adversities and finding a way to use them to the glory of God. It is through that strength, that character that we are able to see beyond ourselves to the goodness and glory of God. It is that kind of character that will lead us towards better relationships with other people and with God.

We need to think hard about our character, about what others see in us, because whether we wish to believe it or not, we show our character every day to those around us. Whether our character is good or poor, others see it. They see it in the way we react to circumstances at work or school. They see it by the way that we react to finances, relationships, car problems, traffic, hunger, worries, gas prices, political campaigns, everything. Matthew 5:14–16 reads, "You are the light of the world. A city on a hill cannot be hidden. Neither do people light a lamp and put it under a bowl. Instead they put it on its stand, and it gives light to everyone in the house. In the same way, let your light shine before men, that they may see your good deeds and praise your Father in heaven."

We are to be a light to the world. This means that our character must be pure, and founded on the bedrock of Christ. Good or bad, we cannot hide our character. If you really want to know what kind of character you have, examine yourself when no one is looking.

Let me share a poem with you.

"Of Character Like Christ" by Dana H. Burnell

Sometimes I stumble Lord and fall.
I fail to give to you my all.
I fail to do the things I should,
and fail to try the way I could.

My character begins to fade.
My light grows dim, I turn to shade.
It's then my gracious God I need,
renewing from your Precious Seed.

I need your light to see the way
to gently guide me through this frey,
so I'll have strength to work Your plan,
the character to be Your man.

Maybe you have thought about your own personal character and how you are perceived by others. Perhaps you've looked at the adversities in your life through your looking glass and seen that you don't have the character that you want to have. Perhaps you realized that your adversities are not being used to glorify God, but to help sustain your own self interests and personal pity party. God can make a difference. God can help. God can take your cares. In Matthew 28 Jesus says, "Come to me, all you who are weary and burdened, and I will give you rest. Take my yoke upon you and learn from me, for I am gentle and humble in heart, and you will find rest for your souls. For my yoke is easy and my burden is light."

Lay your burdens at His feet and bask in the strength of character found only in the love of God, through Christ.

If you haven't yet put on Christ in baptism, why are you waiting? Today is the best day to begin.

Chapter 7

Christian Worship

*P*salm 84:10–12 reads, "Better is one day in your courts than a thousand elsewhere; I would rather be a doorkeeper in the house of my God than dwell in the tents of the wicked. For the LORD God is a sun and shield; the LORD bestows favor and honor; no good thing does He withhold from those whose walk is blameless. O LORD Almighty, blessed is the man who trusts in you."

Ask your children, "How do you get to Church on the Lords' Day?" "Do you get there by accident?" "Did you know on Saturday that you were going to Church on Sunday?" We don't just come to Church, we plan for it. We set aside that time to come together and worship God. Ask them what happens when you get here? "Do your parents ever have to

scold you for talking or making noise in Church?"
"How about getting after you to pay attention or
sing?" When we come to Church it isn't to watch
television, or play with toys, it's to worship God.
We know that there are things we should do in wor-
ship. We learn about what those things are through
the Word of God.

As adults, why do we come together and wor-
ship? Is it because it makes us feel good? Perhaps.
Is it because we get to socialize? Perhaps. Is it
because we love God? It should be. We are com-
manded to worship God. One example is found in
Second Kings 17:35–36 which reads, "When the
LORD made a covenant with the Israelites, He com-
manded them: 'Do not worship any other gods or
bow down to them, serve them or sacrifice to them.
But the LORD, who brought you up out of Egypt
with mighty power and outstretched arm, is the one
you must worship. To Him you shall bow down and
to Him offer sacrifices.'"

God has commanded us to worship Him. Mat-
thew 4:10 Jesus says, "Away from me, Satan! For
it is written: 'Worship the Lord your God, and
serve him only.'" In the beginning, we worshipped
Him because we wanted to. Genesis 4:24–26 says,
"Adam lay with his wife again, and she gave birth
to a son and named him Seth, saying, 'God has
granted me another child in place of Abel, since
Cain killed him.' Seth also had a son, and he named

him Enosh. At that time men began to call on the name of the LORD."

In this chapter I want to examine three aspects of our worship to God. Ready; have we prepared for worship, and what does that mean to prepare for worship? Set; are we there, alert in mind and Spirit when we worship? Go; are we participating in worship the way God would have us participate?

Ready

Exodus 19:10–14 reads, "And the LORD said to Moses, 'Go to the people and consecrate them today and tomorrow. Have them wash their clothes and be ready by the third day, because on that day the LORD will come down on Mount Sinai in the sight of all the people. Put limits for the people around the mountain and tell them, "Be careful that you do not go up the mountain or touch the foot of it. Whoever touches the mountain shall surely be put to death. He shall surely be stoned or shot with arrows; not a hand is to be laid on him. Whether man or animal, he shall not be permitted to live." Only when the ram's horn sounds a long blast may they go up to the mountain.' After Moses had gone down the mountain to the people, he consecrated them, and they washed their clothes."

The Israelites being led by Moses really had to prepare to worship God. There was a lot they had to do. Do you think He requires any less of us today?

Let me share a story with you.

I interviewed for a new position at work once. Preparation was key. In order to get ready for that series of interviews, I studied up on what the people were doing in this new group. I made a list of questions that I wanted to ask each interviewer based on the work that they did and how they fit into the organization. I prayed about the interview process and for guidance and clarity from God. I wore my nicest shirt. I had a pre-meeting with a human resources representative. I prepared. I went out of my way to do extra things to make sure that I could present myself at my best in this interview.

As I was looking at examples of preparation, I found a web site with a list of things to do before you go on a trip. Pay the rent; balance your checkbook; wash your clothes; wash the dishes; clean your house; change the message on your answering machine; confirm airline tickets; shave; plant care; pet care; empty refrigerator of perishables; empty the trash; cut your hair; visit the dentist; get a manicure; unplug electronic devices; forward newspaper; stop mail. Going on a trip takes a lot of preparation.

How many of you watched sports this week? Lots of us followed our favorite teams or players. Do you think they got lucky and just happened to win their perspective contests? Was it an accident that they scored home runs, or goals, or baskets, or whatever way your favorite sport measures points? Do you think your sports hero's were just lucky to have jerked at the right time an in the right way to score? Of course not. They practiced, and planned, and schemed, and determined, and fought, and struggled, and learned, and overcame, and grew, and sweat, and worked, and studied, and toiled, and tried, and prepared, to play sports at their best. Being a great athlete takes preparation.

Isn't our worship to God more important than a sporting event? Isn't our worship to God more important than making sure you get a haircut before a vacation? Isn't our worship to God more important than a business meeting? Why is it then, that we do so little to prepare for it?

We come to Church, sometimes barely on time, and lucky to make it out of bed and get our teeth brushed. We come down the road exceeding the speed limit a bit because we're running late. We figure out how much to put in the offering and hurriedly write a check as the offering plate comes down the isle. We plan and purpose for the things that God is in control of anyway, and neglect planning for the only thing we can control, our love and worship to our almighty God.

So, what does it mean to prepare for worship? It's easy to see how some people prepare for worship. The preacher needs to prepare a lesson, the song leader needs to pick out some songs, and the man that heads the table needs to find something to say, or a scripture to read. At another level it becomes harder, the man offering the opening prayer. Well, he ought to think about it before he gets up there. And finally at our level, the individual, how in the world do we prepare for worship?

I believe that to adequately prepare for worship as an individual you need to do three things:

Put on the right Attitude.

Exodus 3:5–6 reads, "'Do not come any closer,' God said. 'Take off your sandals, for the place where you are standing is holy ground.' Then He said, 'I am the God of your father, the God of Abraham, the God of Isaac and the God of Jacob.' At this, Moses hid his face, because he was afraid to look at God."

Second Samuel 12:20 says, "Then David got up from the ground. After he had washed, put on lotions and changed his clothes, he went into the house of the LORD and worshiped."

Job 1:20 states, "At this, Job got up and tore his robe and shaved his head. Then he fell to the ground in worship."

In each case, these men had an attitude about their worship; they had an attitude of reverence towards the God they were worshipping.

Prayer and meditation to put yourself in the right mindset.

Colossians 4:2–4 states, "Devote yourselves to prayer, being watchful and thankful. And pray for us, too, that God may open a door for our message, so that we may proclaim the mystery of Christ, for which I am in chains. Pray that I may proclaim it clearly, as I should." This shows that you should pray for the message.

Joshua 1:8 reads, "Do not let this Book of the Law depart from your mouth; meditate on it day and night, so that you may be careful to do everything written in it."

Self examination

First Corinthians 11:28–29 says, "A man ought to examine himself before he eats of the bread and drinks of the cup. For anyone who eats and drinks without recognizing the body of the Lord eats and drinks judgment on himself."

Matthew 5:21–24 states, "You have heard that it was said to the people long ago, 'Do not murder, and anyone who murders will be subject to judgment.' But I tell you that anyone who is angry with his brother will be subject to judgment. Again, anyone who says to his brother, 'Raca,' is answerable to the Sanhedrin. But anyone who says, 'You fool!' will be in danger of the fire of hell. Therefore, if you are offering your gift at the altar and there remember that your brother has something against you, leave your gift there in front of the altar. First go and be reconciled to your brother; then come and offer your gift."

We need to come to church prepared to worship God. We need to work during the rest of the week to make that preparation happen. We need to pray, and meditate, and examine ourselves to make sure that we are able to worship, and fix those things that may be a hindrance. Finally, we need to come to church with the right attitude. We are here for the purpose of worshipping the most Holy God, the Creator of all that is, the Master of the universe, and the one who gave us His Son so that we could receive forgiveness.

Set

Now that you have prepared, are you here in mind and soul? Are you poised and prepared and truly worshipping in Spirit and Truth?

Let me share another story with you.

Sometimes even with the best of preparation, people have an off day. When I was in college in Colorado, I had a final exam coming up in my statistics class. The key to this test was a grid of four kinds of formulas. I worked for about a week studying and preparing. The day before the test, I sat in the Student Commons with a friend of mine for several hours, and we grilled each other on that material. I knew it inside and out, upside and down. The next day, I went to take the test and was a bit overconfident. I switched the columns around in the grid of formulas and ended up with a 26% on the test. Thankfully my instructor gave me grace when I explained what had happened. He re-graded it and gave me a C instead of flunking me.

Aren't we like that sometimes when it comes to worship? Even though we have tried, and prepared, and readied ourselves, we get here and we are not really in tune with worship?

I know sometimes when I'm at worship I'm thinking about work. Sometimes I think about lunch. Sometimes I think about the weather, or the view out the window. Sometimes I am just not there worshiping God with all my mind.

But it's really more than a matter of paying attention. It's a matter of having the hunger and desire to truly know God. We sing a song by Marton Nystrom that talks about how we should feel. "As the deer pants for the water, so my soul longs after you. You alone are my hearts desire and I long to worship you." We need to have that hunger and longing ourselves to be worshiping God because we love Him and because we are thankful for all that He has done for us.

Matthew 5:6 tells us, "Blessed are those who hunger and thirst for righteousness, for they will be filled."

Several times in Scripture Jesus says, "He who has ears to hear, let him hear." I think that Jesus is saying that we need to pay attention to God, listen to Him. It's hard to do that when our mind is hungering or thirsting towards other things.

The culmination of our worship is not the lesson. It's not the songs that we sing. It's not the opening or closing prayer. The focal point of our worship is the partaking of the Lords supper. First Corinthians 11:23–26 reads, "For I received from the Lord what I also passed on to you: The Lord Jesus, on the night He was betrayed, took bread, and when He had given thanks, He broke it and said, 'This is my body, which is for you; do this in remembrance of me.' In the same way, after supper He took the cup, saying, 'This cup is the new covenant in my blood; do this, whenever you drink it, in remembrance of me. For whenever you eat this bread and drink this cup, you proclaim the Lord's death until He comes.'"

The culmination of our worship is the celebration that we partake in to remember and focus on the sacrifice of Christ. We are to remember, recall, replay, and concentrate on this sacrifice. We are to be moved, and touched by this gift. We are to think about what it meant for God to give His only Son, Jesus, knowing that sinful mankind would mistreat Him and put Him to death, for our sake. We are to contemplate the enormity of that gift, the wonder of that promise, and the awesomeness of that portrayal of love.

It's hard to focus on the Lord when you're physically hungry and worrying about lunch. It's hard to focus on the Lord when you're worried about writing a check for the offering. It's hard to focus on the Lord when you're being impatient and waiting for the sermon to end. It's hard to focus on the Lord when you're really not mentally present.

We need to come to church and be focused on the worship that we are giving to God. We need to understand that we are coming to give our worship to God, and He is here to receive it. We need to worship the Lord our God with all our hearts, and all our minds, and all our soul (Matthew 22:37).

Go

Not only do we need to prepare, and to be mentally involved in worship, we also need to participate.

Let me share another story with you.

Darin was a good kid. He was a track star. All through high school Darin was the best runner in his school. He broke many records and ran in several events. Darin was a champion, destined for great things. He was being looked at by several colleges and had several possible scholarships waiting in the wings. Darin ran his best for several years. He won every race that he was in during his senior year, and now he made it to the state finals. Darin had a lot going for him.

Darin had a problem though. He had gotten so used to winning that he forgot the things that got him there. He began to believe that it was all natural talent and that he was unbeatable. His coach was working with him and trying to set him straight and explain to him that there was no substitute for hard work and practice. But Darin was listening to his coach less and less as the season went on.

The day before the race, he got into a huge argument with his coach who had planned out a light day for Darin. The coach wanted Darin to rest up a bit before the day of the race. Darin would not listen. Finally, the argument got so intense that Darin quit the team. The coach pleaded with him not to quit but Darin would not listen. After all, he didn't feel that he needed a coach.

The following two days the competition went on. Several people that were not expected to win, had the chance and won, because Darin was not there. The colleges gave the scholarships to the winners, but not Darin. The victory chants went up for the other runners, but not Darin. You can't win, you can't strive, and you can't get the glory or gain the experience or feel the rush if you don't participate.

Second Timothy 2:4–7 says, "No one serving as a soldier gets involved in civilian affairs—he wants to please his commanding officer. Similarly, if anyone competes as an athlete, he does not receive the victor's crown unless he competes according to the rules. The hardworking farmer should be the first to receive a share of the crops. Reflect on what I am saying, for the Lord will give you insight into all this."

When we discuss participation in worship what does that really mean?

There are some things that are obvious. It's easy to understand how the preacher participates. It's easy to think about how the song leader participates. What about the men that are at the table, but don't offer a prayer? Do they participate in the same way as those that do offer public prayer? What about us when we sit in the pew and don't take part in the public workings of the service. How do we participate?

How do we participate in prayer? There are many examples of prayer in Scripture. In the great majority of those examples prayer was a personal experience that the believer shared alone with God. In some examples though, Scripture shows us that people offered public prayer, prayer offered by one person aloud while in a group of people. It doesn't tell us, what the other people in the group were doing while the prayer was going on. However, we do know that prayer is communication with God, and when a man gives a public prayer he is talking to God on behalf of the congregation.

If this were someone other than God, if this were a business meeting, and someone were speaking on behalf of the group, we would be reacting in agreement, and affirming that what he was saying was true. We would be participating by also speaking with agreements and acknowledgments. That's what we should be doing in public prayer. Acknowledging the words that the man offering the prayer is offering. We should be praying too.

Sometimes we listen to a prayer and don't really understand that the prayer is being offered on behalf of the entire congregation. We think we need to come up with our own prayers, and that's ok. But the fact is, public prayer in worship is a time for us all to pray to God. It just so happens that some man has the privilege of doing the public part of this prayer and is acting as our spokesman.

What other things do we do in worship? We sing. How are we to participate in singing? Ephesians

5:19–20 tells us, "Speak to one another with psalms, hymns and spiritual songs. Sing and make music in your heart to the Lord, always giving thanks to God the Father for everything, in the name of our Lord Jesus Christ." Colossians 3:16 states, "Let the word of Christ dwell in you richly as you teach and admonish one another with all wisdom, and as you sing psalms, hymns and spiritual songs with gratitude in your hearts to God."

In both of these passages it doesn't say, "if you sing." It implies that you are to sing. We are commanded to sing (Ephesians 5:19). Now I know that some will say that they can't carry a tune, but if the Holy Spirit can interpret for us to God groanings about things we can't even put into words (Romans 8:26), I think He can help the sound of our songs. If we are not singing we are not obeying the words of God in Scripture. It is sin not to sing in worship. But it's more than just a lack of participation. Singing is to be done to God, in admiration of Him and appreciation of Him. Ephesians 5:19–20 says that we are making music in our hearts to the Lord, giving thanks. That part of the verse is sometimes taken as justification not to sing with our mouths. It doesn't exempt us from singing; it explains the heart that we need to have behind our singing.

How do we participate when we are listening to the sermon? You are listening, right? Is the sermon even really worship at all? The examples in

Scripture of the activities of New Testament worship include someone reading Scripture and teaching. The purpose of this is to teach the message of the Gospel.

Romans 10:13–14 says, "Everyone who calls on the name of the Lord will be saved. How then, can they call on the one they have not believed in? And how can they believe in the one of whom they have not heard? And how can they hear without someone preaching to them?" Romans 10:17 tells us that "faith comes from hearing the message of God." But there is more than just hearing it. As we sit in worship we each have a responsibility to make sure that what is taught is truth.

Acts 17:11 tells us, "Now the Bereans were of more noble character than the Thessalonians, for they received the message with great eagerness and examined the Scriptures every day to see if what Paul said was true." In order to understand the Gospel and determine if the words that are spoken and preached are true, you need to listen. I ask my children what the sermon was about. It is really important that they listen, that we all listen, not draw pictures or read the congregational bulletin.

How do we participate in Communion? As we discussed earlier, we need to remember Christ and the sacrifice. We need to contemplate the generosity of our God and His gift, and we need to set our minds on the things above.

Let me share a poem with you.

"As I Worship my Lord" by Dana H. Burnell

As I bow and worship you oh Lord my God
I pray that I've prepared my heart and mind.
As I sing my songs of praise to you my Lord,
I pray the Spirit works so they sound fine.

As I listen to a portion of Your Word,
I pray I can correctly know Your Truth,
And as I partake of Your memorial feast,
I pray that I approach you as a youth.

As I prepare all week for us to meet,
I pray I think of all I need to do.
But most of all oh Lord my God,
I pray my worship truly pleases you.

Perhaps you've read this chapter and realize that you're not participating in worship or taking it as seriously as you should. Maybe you know that your worship isn't from the heart. Ask your Christian family to pray for you today that your heart may be strengthened and that your load may be lightened.

If you don't know Christ, and haven't put Him on in baptism, I encourage you to do that today.

Chapter 8

God's Grace and Peace

*H*ave you ever had a life changing experience? An experience that so rocked you and so made you challenge yourself that it seemed you needed to really re-examine who you were and what you stood for? An experience where you took an honest look at yourself and your life and said, "Hey it's not all that great." "I've got some things to work on."

It's this kind of experience from which was borne this chapter. It's this kind of path altering jolt, that kind of turmoil that inspired the words below.

As you read this, I'd like you to reach really deep into yourselves and be really, really honest. I'd like you to pay close attention to your conscious and how it reacts to the question I am about to ask you.

I'd like you to consider carefully and wholeheartedly, your response.

Are you completely sure that you are saved and going to Heaven? Did you hesitate in your response? If so, why? We do that, though, don't we? We tiptoe around declaring our salvation. Even at the Lords' table, we talk about the "hope" of eternal life. Hope nothing! God wants us to have the "assurance" of eternal life. God wants us to be sure of our salvation and our future with Him.

Many scriptures plainly state this fundamental truth. "Therefore, my brothers, be all the more eager to make your calling and election sure (Second Peter 1:10)." "Now faith is being sure of what we hope for and certain of what we do not see (Hebrews 11:1)." "We want each of you to show this same diligence to the very end, in order to make your hope sure (Hebrews 6:11)." "But in your hearts set apart Christ as Lord. Always be prepared to give an answer to everyone who asks you to give the reason for the hope that you have (First Peter 3:15)." This scripture has always bothered me. I think that the translation does not do itself justice. The Greek word here for hope is "elpis" which means to anticipate with pleasure, expectation, and "confidence."

I've often wondered why we do this to ourselves. Why we shortchange our Lord and wonder about our salvation. From my own experience it's either because we don't know the bigness of our Lord well enough, or we don't understand the grace of God fully enough.

"Grace and Peace to you . . ."

Pick any of Paul's letters and they all have in the greeting somewhere the phrase, "Grace and peace to you." Most have "Grace and peace to you from God our Father and the Lord Jesus Christ." God wants us to have "grace and peace." He wants us to experience the peace that comes from fully knowing that our election, our salvation is secure, assured, and paid for. But too many times we fail to understand that what we can't do, God can. We fail to see the "bigness" of Jesus, and walk around with an "oh I failed again" attitude thinking that God cannot possibly forgive someone like me, or God cannot possibly forgive me again.

I'd like to introduce you to my Jesus! He's taller than Mount Everest. He's wider than the heavens. He's more powerful than Superman. He's grander than the Grand Canyon. He's mightier than Mighty Mouse. He's deeper than the oceans. He's stronger than Arnold Schwartsinager, smarter than Albert Einstein, tougher than Mike Tyson. He's more loving than Mother Theresa, and more peaceful than Mahatma Ghandi.

My Jesus is able to clean better than All Temp-a-Cheer. He's able to save better than any medication.

He's sustains better than a Snickers candy bar. He relieves pain better that Tylenol. He holds better than Super Glue, heals better than Band Aids, hears better than Miracle Ear, and handles us better than we ever could.

We need to know Him like that!

My Jesus is omniscient. There isn't anything that He doesn't know. He's omnipotent; there isn't anything that He cannot do. He's omnipresent. There isn't anywhere that He does not exist. He's infinite, there isn't any time that He has not, is not, or will not be. My Jesus is everything.

We need to know him like that!

But sadly, we so often sell our Savior short. We think and say things like: "God couldn't possibly love someone like me." "God couldn't possibly forgive me again." "God couldn't possibly overlook something that big." "God couldn't possibly see it the way I do." "Jesus couldn't possibly understand how I feel." "Jesus couldn't possibly have been tempted like this." "Jesus couldn't possibly heal that kind of tear in a relationship." "Jesus couldn't possibly have died for me." "The Holy Spirit couldn't possibly live in someone as weak as me." "The Holy Spirit couldn't possibly help me through this." "The Holy Spirit couldn't possibly give me strength for that." "The Holy Spirit couldn't possibly be still in my life after all the times I've failed Him."

I am here to tell you that, "couldn't possibly," are not words that describe my God! They're not words that describe my Savior! They're not words that describe the Spirit within me!

We need to know him like that!

Romans 5:8 tells us, "But God demonstrates his own love for us in this: While we were still sinners, Christ died for us."

I didn't truly understand that for a long time. I thought it was talking about mankind being still sinful in nature, and Christ died knowing that people would still sin. Although that is the idea, we don't make it personal enough. Christ is omniscient, He knows everything, and He's eternal, He knows history past, present, and future. We can never say, "God can't possibly forgive me again" because He already did! When you became a Christian, God knew every time you would stumble, every time you would make mistakes, every sin you would ever commit, the things you did last week, the things your going do tomorrow, and the things you're going to do next year. Yet He still held out His gift of grace in Christ. There is a gospel song written by Donna Douglas and Pam Thumb, called "He Still Came." It contains the line, "Knowing all He would endure, He still came." Knowing all you would do, God still offered you His grace.

Because of this knowledge of God's grace, this understanding of His love and deliverance, we can no longer say, "God can't possibly . . ." because God already did! If the almighty, all powerful God can have the kind of faith in us to extend His offer of grace to us knowing all the struggles and failures that we will have in the future, we should be open enough to see the enormity of that gift, be humbled by the thought that God wants us anyway, and have "assurance" in our salvation!

Remember, God is big! Bigger than we can even imagine.

The second thing we do is mistakenly believe that perhaps "grace never really reached me." "The baptism never worked or I didn't really receive the gift of the Holy Spirit, because I still struggle with sin, temptation, or suffering."

Let me share a story with you.

When I became a Christian, I smoked cigarettes. I believed that smoking was a sin, and I worked hard to quit. In fact I quit every Monday for six years. I never became fully immersed in the family of God, because I didn't want them to know that I hadn't quit. I didn't want to stay for potlucks or participate in Church activities because after two or so hours of class and worship, I would need a cigarette so badly that I was almost physically sick. I went for six years wondering if I was truly saved. Six years wondering why the Holy Spirit was not keeping me from this. Six years thinking that I must be a lesser Christian, or a failure, because I couldn't quit. Eventually I quit. God knew when I was baptized what kind of a trial this would be for me, and He knew the outcome.

I enjoy the words in Romans 7:14–25. They read, "We know that the law is spiritual; but I am unspiritual, sold as a slave to sin. I do not under-stand what I do. For what I want to do I do not do, but what I hate I do. And if I do what I do not want to do, I agree that the law is good. As it is, it is no longer I myself who do it, but it is sin living in me. I know that nothing good lives in me, that is, in my sinful nature. For I have the desire to do what is good, but I cannot carry it out. For what I do is not the good I want to do; no, the evil I do not want to do—this I keep on doing. Now if I do what I do not want to do, it is no longer I who do it, but it is sin living in me that does it. So I find this law at work: When I want to do good, evil is right there with me. For in my inner being I delight in God's law; but I see another law at work in the members of my body, waging war against the law of my mind and making me a prisoner of the law of sin at work within my members. What a wretched man I am! Who will rescue me from this body of death? Thanks be to God—through Jesus Christ our Lord!"

Paul struggled with sin. We don't know for sure whether he was talking of a specific sin or the general struggle that mankind has with sin. We do know that every sin, from gossip, to smoking, to adultery, to murder is equally sin in God's eyes. We can determine this from the lists of sin in Scripture and the term "and the like" found at the end of one such list in Galatians 5:19–21. We need to understand that God's grace overcomes sin. Paul goes on to say that we still need to make sure we are struggling with sin, and not giving in to it (Romans, chapter eight). We need to remember that we are in a spiritual war and that temptation and sin will always be right around the corner. Sometimes we are going to be overtaken. Getting back on the trail and marching ever towards the finish line is what's important. Paul says this in Second Timothy. In chapter four, verses 6–8 it reads, "For I am already being poured out like a drink offering, and the time has come for my departure. I have fought the good fight, I have finished the race, I have kept the faith. Now there is in store for me the crown of righteousness, which the Lord, the righteous Judge, will award to me on that day—and not only to me, but also to all who have longed for his appearing."

I have struggled with the idea that good Christian people can go through suffering either because of some sort of trauma, or some illness, and God seemingly allows it. Haven't you ever wondered how God's grace plays in to the lives of good Christian people afflicted and suffering? How about the Christian newlyweds that are struggling to get to know each other and finding out that it's not going to be all so rosy? How can good Christian families struggle with financial problems? How come some of us get laid off of our jobs? Why are some God fearing families afflicted with disease or illness? How can children born to Christian mothers and fathers have birth defects? Why do some young people struggle with their grades? How is it that some of the elderly struggle to get out of bed in the morning? Why are there the lonely, the hungry, the homeless, the helpless, the downtrodden, the overlooked, the under loved, the abused, the scared, the poor, the sick, the crippled, the dying, among Christians?

We can say things like, "Surely these kinds of people must have 'hidden sin' in their lives, or they must not truly be saved" or "The Holy Spirit is really not working in their lives, so their baptism never took." And we wonder what is wrong with these people that they are going through this?

Isn't that what Job's friends said about Him? "Man what have you done to make God so mad at you?" "You'd better repent while you still can (Job 34:31–33)."

In Second Corinthians, chapter 12, verses 7–10, Paul talks about his own problem. He says, "To keep me from becoming conceited because of these surpassingly great revelations, there was given me a thorn in my flesh, a messenger of Satan, to torment me. Three times I pleaded with the Lord to take it away from me. But He said to me, 'My grace is sufficient for you, for my power is made perfect in weakness.' Therefore I will boast all the more gladly about my weaknesses, so that Christ's power may rest on me. That is why, for Christ's sake, I delight in weaknesses, in insults, in hardships, in persecutions, in difficulties. For when I am weak, then I am strong."

It's easy for me to understand that passage with regards to sin, but difficult to understand it in terms of a physical problem. There are several ideas about Paul's particular problem, the most common idea being that the "thorn in the flesh" that Paul speaks of is a problem with his eyesight. How in the world can God's grace be sufficient for that? How does that thought even make sense?

Let me share a story with you.

Grace is unmerited favor, unearned parole, unjust lack of punishment. When we lived in Colorado, I bought my wife a new car. We bought it in Scottsbluff Nebraska from my brother-in-law. It was an Oldsmobile Toronado. We had driven a car with a six cylinder engine for quite a while. This car had a fast V8 engine.

The evening that we bought it, we went to Hemmingford, a town about 60 miles north of

Scottsbluff. My wife's sister and her family lived there. On the way there I decided to try the new V8. There were no cars around us and it was a lonely two-lane country road. So I quickly accelerated by pressing the gas pedal to the floor. The car jerked into life and sprinted off like a race car. It was exhilarating.

In a moment the fun faded. As I looked into my rearview mirror I saw the lights of a Nebraska State Patrolman. I knew I had been caught speeding and that I was going to get a ticket. I stopped and rolled down my window and the Officer asked me to bring my license and registration back to his patrol car. I obliged.

Back in his car he proceeded to tell me that I was doing 80 in a 55. He began to write out my ticket and then confirmed the address on my driver's license. I explained that the address was changed and the update was on the back. We lived in Colorado at that time, and when you change addresses, they simply update a sticker and put it on the back of your license until it's time to renew your license.

The Officer had already written the address in, so he stopped and tore up the ticket. It needed to have the correct address and so he had to start over. It was then that he realized that he was out of tickets. He had exhausted his pad of tickets and didn't have another one in the car. He swore a little and told me that I was very lucky. He let me go without a ticket. I deserved one, I should have gotten one, but I didn't.

The funny part is I didn't argue with him. I didn't offer to wait while he went and got some more tickets. I didn't agree to follow him back to the station so he could issue me one there. I took the grace that happened upon me and was appreciative of it. It didn't matter to me that I was lucky. It didn't matter to me that I was undeserving of this fortune. All that mattered was that I got off without a ticket. Nothing else mattered.

God has given us His grace, His promise of eternity! What else can possibly matter?

Philippians 4:4–7 reads, "Rejoice in the Lord always. I will say it again: Rejoice! Let your gentleness be evident to all. The Lord is near. Do not be anxious about anything, but in everything, by prayer and petition, with thanksgiving, present your requests to God. And the peace of God, which transcends all understanding, will guard your hearts and your minds in Christ Jesus."

Knowing that God is big and grace is all that matters, we can certainly accept the Grace and Peace that Paul suggests so often.

Let me share another story with you.

I have Parkinson's disease. Parkinson's slows you down with stiffness and fatigue. Because of this everything takes longer and your productive time during a day becomes less. I have always believed in the proverb, "If a man doesn't work, neither shall he eat." My father was a great worker and he taught me a strong work ethic. I'm also a "type A" personality. I thrive on words like best, fastest, strongest, best quality, customer satisfaction, etc. I have always gone to school, and have been working on my PhD. I was people manager of 50 people and I worked at a large, highly competitive, software company.

When Parkinson's started to cut into my life, I didn't know how to take it, so I buried my self in my work. I knew how to work hard and be successful, and I knew that I could find satisfaction in that. I was looking for peace.

A few months after I was diagnosed I walked the halls at work sure that I was going to fall over. Parkinson's disease and my workaholic reaction to coping with it had gotten the best of me. I knew something had to change. I was looking for peace.

My Doctor said that I needed to cut back to 40 hours a week. I believed that it wouldn't be a problem and gave it a try. That week I delegated a lot of work and I skipped a number of meetings. I cut my hours down to 53. I could see that cutting back was going to be difficult.

I sat down with my wife Kathryn, and we went over my hours. I was working 10 or 12 hours a day at work and a couple of hours in the evening reading email from home. In addition, I was working six hours off and on Saturday, and a couple on Sunday afternoon, all from home. I added them up and it was over 80 hours. I quickly pointed out to Kathryn, and even circled on the white board, the hours that I worked from home. "These don't feel like work," I said. "They do to us" Kathryn replied. It reminded me of Nathan and his statement "David, you're the man (Second Samuel 12:7)." I was convicted.

I had always considered men and women that found their identity in their work, people that are workaholics, people that put their family behind work, as people that had their priorities all messed up. Parkinson's disease helped me to realize that these were descriptions of myself.

So I made some changes. I took six weeks off of work, and did a lot of prayer. I studied and read the Word of God. I talked to a psychologist. I talked to my preacher. I talked to Kathryn. I talked to God. I took stock of life and came to some conclusions. I had been looking for peace. Parkinson's had stolen my peace and I was trying to get it back. It was Paul's

"Grace and Peace" that led me to the conclusions that I thought too small of God and knew too little of grace.

Once I truly understood the strength and power of Jesus, I realized that I don't need to be first, Jesus is. I don't need to be best, Jesus is. I don't need to be fastest. Jesus is. I don't need to be highest. Jesus is. I don't need to be strongest. Jesus is. I don't need to be driven, Jesus is. I don't need a PhD; Jesus is the Doctor of Calvary. I don't need to be the boss; I don't need to be the hero, after all Jesus is all of those things and more!

I don't know about you, but sometimes it seems like we go through life pushing so hard and so fast and so furiously to be on the top of the financial, social, or business ladder that we loose the peace that God intended for us. We forget how big God is and loose the peace that His grace has to offer.

But God gave us grace, and the rest is inconsequential.

Now I work part time, and spend the rest of my day with my family and my God. I'm committed to giving back to my family what I allowed to be taken from them, time with their dad, time with her husband. Priorities are better aligned and I understand grace. For the first time in my adult life, I understood balance. Balance is living in the grace and

Peace that only comes from God. Balance feels good and is an awesome thing.

With the grace of God, nothing else matters. Nothing else matters! Nothing else matters!

"Grace and Peace to you from God our Father and the Lord Jesus Christ (Ephesians 1:1–2)."

Ask yourself the question again. Are you sure that you are saved and bound for Heaven? If you can't immediately raise your hand with confidence, then you need to begin to fix that today. God wants you to have the peace that comes from accepting His grace. He wants you to understand that there are no sins so numerous, no sins so big, no sins so vile, no temptations to strong, to keep Him from you.

Let me share another story with you.

John was a strong Christian man. He lived in a small town in Texas and had a wife and two beautiful children. He was at the beginning of a career in Automobile Sales. John had everything going for him. His Christian life was strong. He and his family attended a little Church with about 80 members. John was the Deacon of finance, and it was assumed that he was destined to be an Elder some day. John was respected and admired. He taught Bible class and lead singing.

The dealership that John worked for had been around for 40 years. It was established and locally owned. As the owner neared retirement, he decided to sell the dealership. He offered it to his best salesman, John. After praying about it and discussing it with his wife, John took a loan out and bought the dealership. John was at the top of his game. He had it all, and was destined for great things.

About this time the economy took a tumble. Car sales dropped off to nothing. John soon found himself in financial trouble. So he began to broker cars. He would buy cars for other dealers and make a small amount on each car. All he had to do was the paperwork. It wasn't long until John realized that the cars with better maintenance records sold more readily and he could make a little more money on them. John began making the cars look "a little better" than he knew they were. He began to write false information into his brokerage deals.

Soon, his dishonesty was discovered. One of John's customers found a huge discrepancy and turned John in to the authorities. John was arrested and sentenced to 180 days in jail, as well as a big fine.

John, the Deacon, the song leader, the Bible class teacher, husband, father, community pillar, and example to all around him had fallen into sin, and paid the price.

Upon his release from jail, John decided to go to Church. He had not stopped attending, and only missed Church while in jail. He was apprehensive of the way that people would react. Some of the same people he had swindled were members of this congregation. Sunday morning as John entered the doors to the sanctuary, he was amazed at what met him. People were friendly. They welcomed him back and hugged him. They expressed how they had prayed for him, and how they loved him and his family.

John went forward at the end of services and asked for the forgiveness of his Church family. He genuinely repented and they genuinely accepted him back. God's family reflects God's love.

There is nowhere that is too far from God. There is nothing too hard for God. There is nothing you can ever do that is too bad, or too big for God to overcome. He wants you to be able to have assurance in your salvation! But, you need to believe that He is able. You need to know the bigness of God.

If the Spirit moves you to draw closer to God, I encourage you to do that today. Perhaps you need prayers. Go to your Church home and ask. They are good people, God's people, and they will help.

Perhaps you can't raise your hand to the question of salvation because you've never developed that saving relationship with God. You can change that today. Remember, God is big and grace is sufficient.

Let me share a poem with you.

"Grace and Peace" by Dana H. Burnell

We all have distractions from our life with God.
We may get discouraged and off the path trod.
At times it may seem like there's no end in sight.
That's when we need to submit to God's light.
God is omniscient, omnipotent too.
There's nothing so ever that God cannot do.
He gave us His Son to atone for our sin.
He opened up Heaven so that we could come in.
God's mercy enables our sorrow to cease.
He gave us His grace, so we'd live in His peace.

You don't need to live a life troubled, tired, weary, scared, lonely, a life outside the fold of God. You don't need to live a life sad, downtrodden, overwhelmed, depressed, concerned or questioning. You don't need to live a life stumbling, looking, longing, hungry or thirsty. You don't need to live another day where you are not able to thrust your hand jubilantly in the air proclaiming that you know you are saved and going to Heaven to be with our God and Savior. Don't live a life without Grace and Peace.

LOVING LIKE
YOU'RE SAVED

As we walk with God, it's important that we emulate God in all we do. First John 4:16 tells us that "God is love." If we are to emulate our Creator we need to be love as well.

As Gods loving people we need to be active in our faith. We are called to be moved by our faith into action (Matthew 2:34–39). Our faith must make us different and spur us on to live lives that are convincing examples of the love of Christ. Loving like you're saved means changing our lives from living our way, to living God's way. It means to put your hand to the plow and do the will of God.

As Gods loving people we need to be living like we are a family. We need to open up to each other, lean on each other, and bear each other's burdens and joys (Galatians 6:2). God never meant for us to go it alone. Worldly pride sometimes keeps us from asking for help. Receiving strength from each other is just as important as giving strength to each other. Loving like you're saved means bearing each others burdens (Galatians 6:2), and sharing each others joys.

As God's loving people we need to realize that He blessed us with many kinds of relationships because He did not want us to be alone (Genesis 2:18). Enjoying those relationships is one way that we can praise and thank God for this wonderful gift. We need to see the gifts of marriage, family, and church family as the blessings they are. We also need to love God with all our heart (Matthew 22:37). Loving like you're saved means loving those around us and the God that made it all possible.

As Gods loving people we need to realize that there are many souls that are lost. We need to understand that Satan is alive and well and hunting as we speak. He is coming like a wolf in sheeps clothing and masquerading as an angle of light (First Corinthians 11:15). Loving like you're saved means helping people to understand the battle that they are in, and learn to fight. Loving like you're saved means fulfilling the great commission, and leading the lost to Christ.

Finally we need to understand the urgency of the Gospel call. We don't know when Christ will return or when we may die. But we do know that they are both facts (Luke 12:40, Hebrews 9:27). Loving like you're saved means understanding the urgency and doing all we can to ensure that we, our friends and family, and everyone we meet are prepared to meet Christ.

Chapter 9

Active Faith

Let me share a story with you.

*R*ichard Jenkins was a hard man. He had lived a hard life, and life had dealt him some hard times. At 22 years old he was arrested and jailed for assault, armed robbery, and attempted murder. He was sentenced to 20 years in prison. While in prison he proved himself to be a cold man. He was placed in solitary confinement on several occasions for violent acts of fighting and assault, and it was even rumored that he had something to do with the mysterious death of another inmate that he had disagreements with.

After 18 years nine months, 11 days, 12 hours and 15 minutes, his day had come. He found himself standing facing a parole board. The parole judge talked at length about his criminal record, and mentioned all of the problems that he had had in jail. The Judge spoke of the solitary confinement Richard had endured, and the socialization problems that he seemed to display.

Finally, the judge told him, "Mr. Jenkins, incarceration is a place where you are to be rehabilitated, to change you old ways, and to learn to be a productive member of society. During your time with us, you have not shown any willingness to change. You have been abusive, obnoxious, and even violent. We can't rehabilitate you all by ourselves. For this to work, you have to want to change. I don't see here any record of your working with us to change your old ways."

Richard, who by this time had become accustomed to living behind bars, slowly stood up, and as he reached into his pocket said this. "You expect a man to be what you expect a man to be." As he pulled out a nickel and a quarter from his pocket, he threw it on the table in front of him and said, "I figure that this is about all the change I'm willing to give you."

Isn't that how we are sometimes? Where all the change we're willing to give to God is what we can toss in the offering plate.

The circumstances of the world today are by and large, in opposition to God. Our lives are inundated with experiences that lead us away from God, experiences that show us and demonstrate to us every day that people don't really fear God. We see around us leaders that are complacent or even wrong about the value and definition of morality, media that brings the unspeakable to prime time nightly news, and stories of children filled with violent images and rage. Today, more than ever we need to have an active faith, faith that moves us and causes us to make a difference. We need to be a positive influence on our world.

James 2:14–26 tells us, "What good is it, my brothers, if a man claims to have faith but has no deeds? Can such faith save him? Suppose a brother or sister is without clothes and daily food. If one of you says to him, 'Go, I wish you well; keep warm and well fed,' but does nothing about his physical needs, what good is it? In the same way, faith by itself, if it is not accompanied by action, is dead. But someone will say, 'You have faith; I have deeds.' Show me your faith without deeds, and I will show you my faith by what I do. You believe that there is one God. Good! Even the demons believe that— and shudder. You foolish man, do you want evidence that faith without deeds is useless? Was not our ancestor Abraham considered righteous for what he did when he offered his son Isaac on the altar? You see that his faith and his actions were working together, and his faith was made complete by what he did. And the scripture was fulfilled that says, 'Abraham believed God, and it was credited to him as righteousness,' and he was called God's friend. You see that a person is justified by what he does and not by faith alone. In the same way, was not even Rahab the prostitute considered righteous for what she did when she gave lodging to the spies and sent them off in a different direction? As the body without the Spirit is dead, so faith without deeds is dead."

James was not even remotely suggesting that we are saved by our works, he was stating the obvious, that the manifestation of what we do, our outward actions, that part of us that people know and relate with speaks volumes about the content and quality of our hearts.

In this chapter we are going to consider the fact that we need to reach out to the world, fulfill the great commission, and bring people to God and God to people. We need to be people of action and truly have our faith make a difference in our world.

Edmund Burke said, "Nothing is so fatal to religion as indifference." Aristotle stated, "In the arena of human life the honors and rewards fall to those who show their good qualities in action."

The question we need to begin with is this, "Is our own personal faith causing us to make a difference in the world around us?"

There are three reasons that we need to consider when calling ourselves Christ's people with an active faith.

Everything is God's

Psalm 24:1–2 reads, "The earth is the Lord's and all it contains, the world and those who dwell in it. For He has founded it upon the seas, and established it upon the rivers."

At an early age I began to give my children an object lesson. Whenever I would find a toy or bicycle or other artifact left out in the yard I would ask them to pick it up. I would stress that we needed to take care of our things, and my children knew the queue. When I asked them whose bike or toy it was, they learned to respond, "God's bike."

Let me share another story with you.

A certain man had one of those day-at-a-time calendars that had a separate tear off paper for every day. Each day, before he went to bed, he would tear off the days date from the calendar and spend a few minutes contemplating it. He would then say a prayer to God thanking him for giving him another precious day, and ending with the thought that he had done the best he could with it. As he crumpled it up and let it fall into the waste bin he would tell God that now he was giving it back to Him.

Everything that we have, from the sunrise to each breath we take is God's, on loan to us. The buildings we congregate in are God's buildings. The congregations we fellowship and worship with are God's congregations. It is out of that love and respect for God that we should want to take great care in every aspect of the things that He has loaned us.

How we take care of something that belongs to someone else is a direct reflection of the love and respect that we have for that other person. We should want to, out of respect for God act to preserve, protect, and uphold the world around us, because it all belongs to God and He has loaned it to us. We should be concerned about what happens to and with all of the things in the world. They all belong to God.

All men are made in God's holy image.

In Genesis 1:26 we read, "And God said, Let us make man in or image, after our likeness . . ." Genesis 5:1 says that "God created man in His likeness." We all are images of God, we all have a share in the holiness and glory of God. All mankind is made in His image.

Another object lesson that I have had with my children involves the way they treat each other. Being siblings, they don't always get along. When they fight we discuss the fact that we are all children of God and all created in His image. So we need to have love, respect, and concern for each other, if only for that reason alone.

First Corinthians 11:7 says that "man should not cover his head because he is the image and glory of God." In Colossians 1:15 it speaks of Christ as being the image of God. All mankind shares with Christ, the holy and glorious image of God. Because of this we should be concerned about what we as a people are doing to that holy image. Are we preserving it and defending it, or are we defiling it?

We should be concerned about what happens to and with all of the people in the world. They belong to God, and are created in His image.

We need to work to fulfill God's Goal—none should be lost.

Second Peter 3:9 says that "The Lord is not slow about His promise, as some count slowness, but is patient towards you, not wishing for any to perish but for all to come to repentance." In Matthew, chapter 28, before Christ ascended into Heaven, He said in verses 19–20, "Go therefore and make disciples of all the nations, baptizing them in the name of the Father, and of the Son and of the Holy Spirit, teaching them to observe all that I commanded you; and lo I am with you always, even to the end of the age."

God has a goal that none should be lost, and He has given us a directive to help carry out that goal. In order to do this we have to act.

What is this action and how do we go about it?

Christ said that the greatest two commandments were to love the Lord our God with all of our heart, mind, and strength, and to love our neighbors as ourselves (Matthew 22:37–39). This action must include this thought. Our action needs to be different than the actions of the people of the world. Scripture says that we are to let our light shine before men (Matthew 5:16).

For a long time I thought that my light shone because of my characteristics. I have a good work ethic, I don't use foul language, and I'm honest. I thought surely that God was reflected by my attributes. However, in Scripture James tells us that even the demons fear or respect God. Likewise I don't think that godly attributes are action enough to bring about change for God. There are a lot of really good people in the world that are not Christian people that have good work ethics, that are honest, that refrain from foul language. That just simply is not enough. We have to be advocates for Christ. Our faith needs to make a difference.

James 1:23–27 tells us, "Anyone who listens to the word but does not do what it says is like a man who looks at his face in a mirror and, after looking at himself, goes away and immediately forgets what he looks like. But the man who looks intently into the perfect law that gives freedom, and continues to do this, not forgetting what he has heard, but doing it—he will be blessed in what he does. If anyone considers himself religious and yet does not keep a tight rein on his tongue, he deceives himself and his religion is worthless. Religion that God our Father accepts as pure and faultless is this: to look after orphans and widows in their distress and to keep oneself from being polluted by the world." This is the action that we need to have, to actively demonstrate love from helping people with their physical needs to helping people with their spiritual needs.

The world is in need of help, and we need to do what it takes to give it. We need to be ready to change the world around us by stepping out of our comfort zones and become what God needs. We need to make a difference. If your faith is not making a difference in the world, what value does it have?

Heaven is a big place and we need to help fill it. Revelation 21:10–16 reads, "And he carried me away in the Spirit to a mountain great and high, and showed me the Holy City, Jerusalem, coming down out of heaven from God. It shone with the glory of God, and its brilliance was like that of a very precious jewel, like a jasper, clear as crystal. It had a great, high wall with twelve gates, and with twelve angels at the gates. On the gates were written the names of the twelve tribes of Israel. There were three gates on the east, three on the north, three on the south and three on the west. The wall of the city had twelve foundations, and on them were the names of the twelve apostles of the Lamb. The angel who talked with me had a measuring rod of gold to measure the city, its gates and its walls. The city was laid out like a square, as long as it was wide. He measured the city with the rod and found it to be 12,000 stadia in length, and as wide and high as it is long."

Let me share a poem with you.

"Faith That Works" by Dana H. Burnell

We live a life of sheltered love, protected by the
    hand of God.
We act as though we are alone, and on no beaten
    path do trod.
Our lives are softly comfortable, surrounded by
    created ease;
we live this life of ours for God and pray on
    bended knees.

But we are not the whole of it, the world's a big
    ger place,

we cannot rest complacently, the worlds in need
    of grace.
The world's not going to come to God, it sits in
    trembling fear,
we need to bring to God the world, the world
    He holds so dear.

Our folly or our labors are the seeds that grow
    this fruit;
our love and our compassion are the waters for
    its root.
We can fret about our own ways, or we can see
    the bigger view,
the world needs God's salvation, spread to all by
    me and you.

From this chapter I'd like you to grasp one idea. We are charged with spreading the good news of Jesus to the world. In order to do that we need to have an active faith, a faith that moves us to make a difference in the world around us. Is your own personal faith causing you to make a difference in the world around you? Think about that as you walk your walk with God. If your faith is not moving you to action, perhaps you could use the prayers of your Christian family.

If you're not yet a part of God's kingdom, I encourage you to be baptized into His fold today. Christ is the only way to an eternity with God.

Chapter 10

Gods' Family

What do you think of when you hear the word "family?" Merriam Webster has several definitions of that word. The first is a group of persons of common ancestry. Many people have grown up in families with a lot of history and background. They can trace their ancestry back several generations. Very close relationships exists in this kind of environment, and the word "family" has very strong blood ties, the blood relationships are very important. We have several examples of those kinds of families in Scripture. Adam, Abraham, Noah, David, these were all part of the same blood line that extended from Adam to Jesus, or perhaps more correctly, to Joseph, the father of Jesus.

Blood line was important because it carried with it a rich tradition, and promises of God.

Then there are people that think of the "family" in a much different way. Webster's' second definition is a group of individuals living under one roof and usually under one head, or a household. That's more in line with my thinking. I was adopted at the age of two and to me "family" doesn't really have anything to do with bloodline. It has to do with relationships. I think this kind of understanding of the word family bridges itself more easily into Webster's third definition which is a group of people united by certain convictions or a common affiliation. I don't have a problem thinking of a close friend as a brother or sister. I also have blood sisters who are family. However the Christian family that I worship with feels more like family than some of my blood relatives.

To others, the word "family" may not bring good memories or feelings. Perhaps you were brought up in a home that was broken or dysfunctional and when you hear the word family it brings back bad memories, or memories that you'd just as soon not remember.

But what is family really? Families are the people that rejoice with you, that cry with you, that pick you up when you fall, and hold you up when you're tired. They are your support system, your helpers in time of need, your encouragers, your refuge, always looking for your best, and always at the ready to lend a hand, or a dollar, or a hug. "Family" means those people that would do anything for you and those that you would do anything for.

Let me share a story with you.

Todd Grady's parents started off like any other young couple, eager, hopeful, and hard working. Todd's dad worked in a plant in Detroit building automobile starters. Todd's mother waited tables at a local restaurant. When Todd came along, they made a decision to have Todd's mom stay at home and Todd's dad took on extra shift work. It wasn't long, working two shifts and feeling really out of place at home, that Todd's dad began to spend more free time with his work buddies. One thing led to another, and soon, Todd's parents got divorced. A bad turn of events at the restaurant and Todd's mother was out of work. On a snowy Michigan evening, she took Todd down to the police station and requested that they help her find a place for him. Todd, now three, went into foster care.

When Todd was five he met Frank. Frank was a student at the time and was working on a degree in Mechanical Engineering. Frank had always felt like he wanted a brother, but never got the opportunity. He had one sister and that was it. So, Frank had heard about, and checked into the Big Brother program. This was a program that matched up a young boy with an older boy so that they could have a "brother" sort of relationship. The commitment was that Frank spend one afternoon or evening a week with his "little brother." Frank signed up and ended up with a boy named Todd.

Frank and Todd hit it off immediately. They found that they could talk to each other, and laugh, and really have a good time. They ended up being pretty inseparable. So much so, that as Todd bounced around from foster home to foster home, they made an exception and allowed Frank to stay in contact. Sometimes they lived close to each other, and at times were as much as 100 miles away. Nevertheless, Frank always found a way to make it to Todd's current home at least twice a week. Frank taught Todd how to overcome his fear of water, and how to swim. He taught him how to ride a bike, and how to be brave when you skinned your knee. Frank taught Todd about algebra and fishing, baseball and pinball, life, love, and patience.

As they both got older, Frank got married. One of the agreements that he made with his wife was that he was going to continue to be a Big Brother to Todd. Todd grew up too. He found that he had questions in life, and regardless of the issue, he knew he could talk to Frank.

They stayed involved in each others life until the end. As an older man, Todd realized that the years didn't so much separate him and Frank, and at Frank's funeral, Todd eyes swelled up with tears as he reminisced. He thought of the relationship he had formed with Frank. Frank was his older brother, his father figure, and his friend. Todd realized that all that he knew about being a man, he learned from Frank. All that he knew about being a husband he had learned from watching Frank's example. Through all the turmoil in Todd's life, all the foster homes, all the questions he about his parents, all the instability, there was always Frank. Todd and Frank were Family.

In the Church we use the word "family" in two ways. We use it to denote the "family" of God, a true blood relationship in which we are all adopted into God's family through Christ and redeemed by Him (Ephesians 1:5–8). We also think of it in terms of human relationships. We call each other "family," use the words "brother" and "sister," and in many ways we treat each other like family. Romans 8:17 tells us, "Now if we are children, then we are heirs—heirs of God and co-heirs with Christ, if indeed we share in his sufferings in order that we may also share in his glory." Second Corinthians 1:7 says, "And our hope for you is firm, because we know that just as you share in our sufferings, so also you share in our comfort." Acts 4:32–34 states, "All the believers were one in heart and mind. No one claimed that any of his possessions was his own, but they shared everything they had. With great power the apostles continued to testify to the resurrection of the Lord Jesus, and much grace was upon them all. There were no needy persons among them. For from time to time those who owned lands or houses sold them, brought the money from the sales and put it at the apostles' feet, and it was distributed to anyone as he had need." Jesus affirms these relationships in Matthew 12:46–50. It reads, "While Jesus was still talking to the crowd, his mother and brothers stood outside, wanting to speak to him. Someone told him, 'Your mother and brothers are standing outside, wanting to speak to you.' He replied to him, 'Who is my mother, and who are my brothers?' Pointing to his disciples, he said, 'Here are my mother and my brothers. For whoever does the will of my Father in heaven is my brother and sister and mother'"

The early Church took very seriously the words of Christ in Mark 12 when He said that the greatest commandment is to "Love the Lord your God with all your heart and with all your soul and with all your mind and with all your strength. The second is this: Love your neighbor as yourself."

Now I'm not advocating that we are to prove that we are family to each other by selling our homes or possessions, even though that is something to think about. What I am saying is that there is ample evidence in Scripture that the Church thought of each other as family.

Talking about members of the Body or the Church having different functions and that we should treat each other respectfully Paul writes in Romans 12:15 "Rejoice with those who rejoice; mourn with those who mourn."

The early Church was also concerned for and took care of the widows and the orphans. James 5:13 says, "Is any one of you in trouble? He should pray. Is anyone happy? Let him sing songs of praise. Is any one of you sick? He should call the elders of the church to pray over him and anoint him with oil in the name of the Lord. And the prayer offered in faith will make the sick person well; the Lord will raise him up. If he has sinned, he will be forgiven. Therefore confess your sins to each other and pray for each other so that you may be healed. The prayer of a righteous man is powerful and effective." Ephesians 6:18–20 reads "And pray in the Spirit on all occasions with all kinds of prayers and requests. With this in mind, be alert and always keep on praying for all the saints. Pray also for me, that whenever I open my mouth, words may be given me so that I will fearlessly make known the mystery of the gospel, for which I am an ambassador in chains. Pray that I may declare it fearlessly, as I should."

Titus 2:1–8 states, "You must teach what is in accord with sound doctrine. Teach the older men to be temperate, worthy of respect, self-controlled, and sound in faith, in love and in endurance. Likewise, teach the older women to be reverent in the way they live, not to be slanderers or addicted to much wine, but to teach what is good. Then they can train the younger women to love their husbands and children, to be self-controlled and pure, to be busy at home, to be kind, and to be subject to their husbands, so that no one will malign the word of God. Similarly, encourage the young men to be self-controlled. In everything set them an example by doing what is good. In your teaching show integrity, seriousness and soundness of speech that cannot be condemned."

There is every precedence in Scripture for us to treat each other like family. The Church worked together and shared. They shared their possessions, their joys and sorrows. They prayed for each other, helped each other in time of need. They taught each other, the old helped the young. They asked each other for help. They ate together. They were a big extended family to each other. They took an active part in each others lives. They were open and they were giving.

Do you feel like the congregation you attend is "family?" Some congregations have a strong history of treating each other like family. When someone lets it be known that they have a need, these congregations jump to the ready taking care of that need. I've seen people helped by their Christian families with all sorts of issues, and

I've personally been on the prayer lists of my church family many times. Congregations like these are the most loving, caring, helping, family kind of places you can ever imagine. It's amazing how these "families" step up to help each other, shoulder adversity together, and show the love of Christ so richly.

I've seen Christian families help others with transportation, food, money, school, sickness, fear, anxiety, problems with sin, problems with strife, problems with marriage, and problems with everything. It's really inspiring to be in a family where so many are so willing to help. Surely Christ dwells in a family like that.

But there is one part that many families aren't so good at. That is letting each other in. It's hard to have a ministry of helping, of prayer and concern, of sorrow and rejoicing, of needs fulfilled if those needs are not made aware. I was part of a Christian family where Sunday evening services grew to become very special. Almost every Sunday there was a baptism, or brothers and sisters came forward and were prayed for. When one was baptized, the entire congregation joined hands in a big circle and sang "We love you with the love of the Lord" to them. It was very special indeed. People were intertwined in each others lives, sharing and shouldering problems together. The times of worship were filled with a feeling of love and peace. But, the fire died down and the fervor subsided. People stopped sharing.

Many will rationalize it away, "those were special times," "the world was different then," "the congregation was smaller then, and I don't know as many people now," "some of the people that sparked that have moved away," "we don't have as many needs as we did back then." Peoples needs don't change that dramatically. People still have needs, but instead of sharing them they are struggling. They are struggling with sin, struggling with marriage or parent-child relationships, struggling with school, or work, finances, friends, family, health, homework, faith, or love. Enough struggling people exist in congregations that if we were all really honest the front two pews would be filled at the invitation call by brothers and sisters that needed the prayers of their family. People aren't as open and willing to let each other in anymore.

Do you wonder why that is? We know we ought to. We understand the seriousness of sin and the reality of Satan. We know that we should find our strength together and that together we need to circle the wagons because this is a war that we are involved in (Ephesians 6:10–12). But we don't. We condition ourselves. We force ourselves to be reserved, or prideful, or closed, or whatever you want to call it because we don't want people to see us as weak, scared, tempted, or in need. If everyone that had a need was honest about it, the invitation would be meaningful and rejuvenating, not uncomfortable and never-ending. Have you ever felt like the invitation was somehow pointed at you, and you could hardly wait until the song was over? Why don't we let each other in?

Sometimes it's fear. We're afraid that someone will think less of us if we admit that we have money or marriage problems. We're afraid that people will snub us if we admit that we struggle with sin. Afraid that we will loose face with the church family if we admit that parenting is hard, or that our friends or coworkers are hard for us to reach. We're afraid that we will be looked down upon if we admit fear or frustration or an inability to cope. We're even afraid that we will look like braggarts if we share our blessings. James 5:16 tells us, "Therefore confess your sins to each other and pray for each other so that you may be healed. The prayer of a righteous man is powerful and effective."

Everyone has or will have problems in money and marriage, they will struggle with sin, they will have problems reaching those close to them, they will experience relationship problems, they will get stuck in a problem they don't know their way out of, they will get frustrated, and they will have joy. It's a shame if we are not able to share our lives with each other.

A second reason that we don't share is that we are too prideful. We say things like "good Christians are also good money managers." "Good Christians don't sin." "Good Christians are able to stand up to Satan." Satan is real and no amount of pride can keep him at bay, in fact that pride is right where he wants us to begin. Then he can get his grips firmly on us. It's detrimental if we're not able to share with each other.

The third reason why we don't share is because we really just don't get it. God wants us to be family, and He wants us to share. He wants us to love each other. First John 3:16 tells us. "This is how we know what love is: Jesus Christ laid down His life for us. And we ought to lay down our lives for our brothers. If anyone has material possessions and sees his brother in need but has no pity on him, how can the love of God be in him? Dear children, let us not love with words or tongue but with actions and in truth. This then is how we know that we belong to the truth, and how we set our hearts at rest in his presence whenever our hearts condemn us. For God is greater than our hearts, and He knows everything." It's a shame if we're not able to share with each other.

Galatians 1:10 reads, "Am I now trying to win the approval of men, or of God? Or am I trying to please men? If I were still trying to please men, I would not be a servant of Christ." When you care what people think, when you worry about your reputation, when you put your pride first, you are seeking the approval of men, not of God. Give it over to God, and He'll take care of the rest.

Let me share a poem with you.

"Let Me In" by Dana H. Burnell

I see the hurt within your eyes, and feel the pain
    within;
I know that you've got battles that you don't
    think you can win.
It doesn't matter what it is, I'll help with all my
    might.
I'll stand behind you or before you, to your left
    or to your right.

I'll hold your hand or hold you up, I'll give to
    you my all.
I won't let you be defeated, I'll hold tight so you
    don't fall.

But I can't hold your hand so tight when you
    keep it to yourself.
I can't help you if you put your problems on a
    shelf.
I see the tears roll down your cheeks. I know
    you're feeling blue.
I'll do my very best to lift you up and see you
    through.

You are my friend, my family. A treasure I hold
    dear.
I'll help you each and every day, if you'll but let
    me near.
But I can't read your mind or heart, and I can't
    heal your woes,

unless I know the problem, so please tell me of
your foes.

I see your head drop in despair. I hear the faint-
est sigh.
Your heart is heavy in your chest, and reveals
you as you cry.
I know that you'd feel better, if you let me take
an ore.
Together we could get this wandering ship into
the shore.

But I can't paddle all alone, if I don't know your
boat.
Please let me take my turn so you can get some
rest afloat.
I see you fall upon your knees and know your
pain is strong,
if only I could help you, that's the thing for which
I long.

Your burdens are too heavy; your baggage is too
big.
Please let me carry something, a stump, a branch,
a twig.
But now I watch you helplessly and know you've
pain within.
But there's not much that I can do, if you won't
let me in.

Wouldn't you pray for a brother or sister that
needed your prayers? Wouldn't you help council
them if they needed help with family relationships
or money problems? Wouldn't you cry with them if

they had sorrow tearing at their heart? Wouldn't you rejoice with them if they had fortune smile on them? Wouldn't you help a brother or sister, no matter the issue, because that's what family does for each other? Why not let them do the same for you?

Who is this family? Would you share your fears, your joys, your sorrows, your problems, your needs with the people in your Christian family? You have the opportunity every time you assemble. You can use your family as God intended, or you can go away and continue to struggle alone. I urge you today, to ask for help with your burdens. If you have sin, ask forgiveness and let it be nailed to the Cross. That's why Christ died, was for the forgiveness of our sins. If you have joy, share it with your family. If you have needs, let them be known to one another.

If you don't have a relationship with Christ yet and haven't put Him on in baptism, I ask, "Why do you wait?" He stands at the door (Revelation 3:20) and awaits you.

Chapter 11

Relationships

$\mathcal{E}$very time I sit down to write, it seems to come at a time when I have had an epiphany, experienced something, or learned something (usually the hard way) that helps me to draw closer to God. It's always an opportunity to share and hopefully to give you something to consider as you walk with God.

One of the reasons that we are put on this earth is to love and care for each other. Jesus said in Matthew 22:39 that the second greatest commandment is to "Love your neighbor as yourself." But we forget to do that, or we are afraid to do that, or we are to prideful or sinful to do that.

Almost all of our relationships can be put into a category called "friends." We are a people created to have friends. Ecclesiastes 6:16 tells us that, "A faithful friend is the medicine of life." Jesus said in John 15:13, "Greater love hath no man than this, to lay down his life for a friend." Emerson said "A friend may be well reckoned the masterpiece of nature." He also said "The only way to have a friend is to be one."

Scripture is full of examples and exhortations to share our sorrows, burdens and joys with each other. Some examples include the following.:

- Ephesians 6:2 tells us, "Carry each other's burdens, and in this way you will fulfill the law of Christ."
- First Timothy 4:18 states, "Therefore encourage each other with these words."
- Hebrews 10:24 relates this, "And let us consider how we may spur one another on toward love and good deeds."
- Ephesians 4:32 says, "Be kind and compassionate to one another, forgiving each other, just as in Christ God forgave you."

I'd like you to think about relationships. I'd like you to consider the most meaningful and fulfilling relationships that you have. Contemplate on those relationships in which you would be willing to commit to a great deal of risk because your trust goes deep enough that you would share your deepest most private thoughts, fears, concerns. Think about what that relationship means to you. Think about how deeply your trust goes, how wide you open your arms for embrace, how high your aspirations are for each other, and how long your relationship will last.

We are meant to be a people of relationships. God has instituted several types of relationships for us to have. God instituted the marriage relationship. The first human relationship established was between Adam and Eve. God didn't want man to be alone on the earth. God is a God of relationships. Genesis 2:18 reads, "The LORD God said, 'It is not good for the man to be alone. I will make a helper suitable for him.'" So God created a helper for man, and they were bonded as the first couple in the human race. We read more detail in Genesis 2:20–24. It says, "But for Adam no suitable helper was found. So the LORD God caused the man to fall into a deep sleep; and while he was sleeping, He took one of the man's ribs and closed up the place with flesh. Then the LORD God made a woman from the rib He had taken out of the man, and He brought her to the man. The man said, 'This is now bone of my bones and flesh of my flesh; she shall be called "woman," for she was taken out of man. For this reason a man will leave his father and mother and be united to his wife, and they will become one flesh.'"

The dictionary definition of marriage is: A close union, intimacy, compatibility, comradeship, friendship.

In Ephesians 5:22–28, Paul defines the way husbands and wives should relate to each other. It says, "Wives, submit to your husbands as to the Lord. For the husband is the head of the wife, as Christ is the head of the Church, His body, of which He is the Savior. Now as the church submits to Christ, so also wives should submit to their husbands in everything. Husbands, love your wives, just as Christ loved the church and gave Himself up for her to make her holy, cleansing her by the washing with water through the word, and to present her to Himself as a radiant Church, without stain or wrinkle or any other blemish, but holy and blameless. In this same way, husbands ought to love their wives as their own bodies. He who loves his wife loves himself."

But the sad thing is that people let each other down. The divorce rate is 50% among non-Christians and Christians alike. Marriage relationships are hard to build and frail to maintain because people let people down.

God also instituted family relationships. He wants us to have relationships on a family level. Family was instituted in Genesis with Adam and Eve. The hierarchy of a family can be found in Colossians 3:18–21. Here it talks about the hierarchy of a family in terms of respect and love. "Wives, submit to your husbands, as is fitting in the Lord. Husbands love your wives and do not be harsh with them. Children, obey your parents in everything, for this pleases the Lord. Fathers, do not embitter your children, or they will become discouraged."

Family relationships are based on love and trust, but sometimes families are what we term "dysfunctional," or messed up. What does that really mean, dysfunctional? Deception, hatred, adultery, murder, incest, children out of wedlock, and fear are all things that can make a family dysfunctional. Jacob's family is a great example because they experienced all of them (Genesis). Family relationships are hard to create and frail to maintain, because people let people down.

God instituted Church Relationships. Acts 2:44–47 shows that there is a definite relationship that exists between believers. That is a relationship based on belief in God. "All the believers were together and had everything in common. Selling their possessions and goods, they gave to anyone as he had need. Every day they continued to meet together in the temple courts. They broke bread in their homes and ate together with glad and sincere hearts, praising God and enjoying the favor of all the people. And the Lord added to their number daily those who were being saved."

Scripture also shows us that as believers we need to strengthen and exhort each other. Titus 2:3–8 says, "Likewise, teach the older women to be reverent in the way they live, not to be slanderers or addicted too much wine, but to teach what is good. Then they can train the younger women to love their husbands and children, to be self-controlled and pure, to be busy at home, to be kind, and to be subject to their husbands, so that no one will malign the word of God. Similarly, encourage the young men to be self-controlled. In everything set them an example by doing what is good. In your teaching show integrity, seriousness and soundness of speech that cannot be condemned, so that those who oppose you may be ashamed because they have nothing bad to say about us."

In fact we are commanded to commit to these relationships; we are to love each other. First John 4:19–21 tells us, "We love because He first loved us. if anyone says, 'I love God,' yet hates his brother, he is a liar. For anyone who does not love his brother, whom he has seen, cannot love God, whom he has not seen. And He has given us this command: Whoever loves God must also love his brother."

But even in the church, the unity sometimes fails. Acts 15:36–40 tells us, "Some time later Paul said to Barnabas, 'Let us go back and visit the brothers in all the towns where we preached the word of the Lord and see how they are doing.' Barnabas wanted to take John, also called Mark, with them, but Paul did not think it wise to take him, because he had deserted them in Pamphylia and had not continued with them in the work. They had such a sharp disagreement that they parted company. Barnabas took Mark and sailed for Cyprus, but Paul chose Silas and left, commended by the brothers to the grace of the Lord." Galatians 2:11 states, "When Peter came to Antioch, I opposed him to his face, because he was clearly in the wrong." Even among Apostles sometimes there is strife. Church relationships are difficult to create, and frail to maintain because brothers and sisters let brothers and sisters down.

Relationships are hard at any level because the world gets in the way and redefines them. It distorts what those relationships should mean in the first place. Spousal commitments are often done as "live together" arrangements. Couples come in any combination of genders. Marriage relationships are twisted by the schemes of Satan. No wonder it's hard to have committed marriage relationships.

Families are not arranged by God's definition, No husband, no wife, no father, two fathers, two mothers, no marriage commitment. The world's view of a family is twisted by the schemes of Satan to be less than God intended it to be. No wonder it's hard to have family relationships.

Church relationships are not what God intended either. We divide over the colors of carpet, the order of worship, the number of communion cups, the style of preaching, personal reputations, self centeredness, pride, and sin. The world's definition of committed church relationships is twisted by the schemes of Satan. No wonder it's sometimes hard to have a close Church relationship.

Satan also confuses our balance of risk and commitment. As society has clamored for information we have deteriorated the meaning of relationships to the point that we produce trash magazines like the National Enquirer, and Star. We want to know intimate details of the lives of people that are well known by their public persona, their fame, and their work. We covet the understanding brought about by trust by betraying that trust through such publications. We want the scoop without having to work for it, or pay the price necessary for real relationships.

Relationships that manifest years of trust and faith aren't produced through happenstance; they don't exist because of good fortune or upbringing. They exist because they were produced as the fruit of a great effort. An effort that took place over a significant amount of time. An effort that was progressively more revealing as trust was built and bonds were formed. If you think about it, there is a bit of risk associated with any relationship, and the deeper the relationship, the greater the risk. When you know someone so well that you confide in them, you put yourself at risk.

Let me share a story with you.

As a ninth grader, I had a crush on one of the "popular" girls. I wrote her a love note thinking that I was sharing with someone that I cared a great deal about. Her reaction was to share it with the rest of her friends, and the next thing I knew I was being laughed at by what I was sure was the entire human race. When I got home that day I told my dad and he gave me a bit of advice. He said, "Don't ever write anything down that you don't want to be made public." I tell you this story to illustrate that committed relationship are two sided. They require effort on the part of both parties. God is always willing. Its man that is reluctant.

Committed relationships are not common. We find ourselves unwilling to pay the cost required to create and maintain those relationships. Even in the Church we don't have as many deep, trusting, unconditional relationships as we could. We're reluctant to commit, and convince ourselves that that the other things that occupy our lives are overwhelmingly more important, so we don't spend the time to create and maintain those relationships.

What are the ingredients in forming such a relationship? Of course there has to be an amount of trust. But even more importantly there has to be experience. You need to experience each other so that you have the common, thoughts, understanding, and memories necessary to have that kind of relationship.

Can you create that kind of relationship with someone at a concert? Probably not. How about when you meet someone in a crowded room? Not likely. How about when you meet someone with their family, perhaps at Church? Not a chance! A chance meeting is not sufficient basis for a committed relationship. The most rewarding, sharing, committed, supportive bonds that we build are not built in a crowd. They're not built in a team. They're not built as a family. They're built one moment at a time. They're built by spending one-on-one time with each other. They are built by spending time alone together.

It's like that in all of our relationships. If we want them to be full of meaning, we have to mean for them to be full. We have to commit to spending private time alone together. As hard as that is it's the key to developing close personal relationships such as marriage or family or our church relationships.

Earlier I said that it was such an experience that inspired my writing here. One of the greatest things that can happen to a relationship is to spend time alone together. I found that in all my trials, in all my victories and all my defeats, all of my dreams and fears, all of the deepest things of my life and mind, I had not spent the time with someone to produce and maintain that relationship at the level it could and should be. I had neglected to spend one on one time alone. You know who I forgot to include, who I neglected to spend time alone with? God.

I said earlier that the first human relationship was between Adam and Eve, but the first relationship of humanity was the relationship between Adam and God. They walked in the garden together and talked. That must have been awesome. Oh how I would have loved to be in Adam's place. In Genesis, chapter two, verses 15 and 16 it reads "The LORD God took the man and put him in the Garden of Eden to work it and take care of it. And the LORD God commanded the man, 'You are free to eat from any tree in the garden; but you must not eat from the tree of the knowledge of good and evil, for when you eat of it you will surely die.'"

Throughout Scripture our hero's of faith spent time alone with God. Abraham spent time alone with God. Genesis 17:1–2 tells us, "When Abram was ninety-nine years old, the LORD appeared to him and said, 'I am God Almighty; walk before me and be blameless. I will confirm my covenant between me and you and will greatly increase your numbers.'"

Genesis 5:24 tells us that, "Enoch walked with God; then he was no more, because God took him away . . ." Imagine being able to say that you walked with God, and that He took you away. Away to where? That must have been incredible.

David spent time alone with God. When David was convicted by Nathan the prophet of murdering Bathsheba's husband so he could have her for himself he penned the Psalm, chapter 51. Verses 10–12 read, "Create in me a pure heart, O God, and renew a steadfast spirit within me. Do not cast me from your presence or take your Holy Spirit from me. Restore to me the joy of your salvation and grant me a willing spirit, to sustain me." It sounds like David was alone with God.

Jesus was our greatest example of spending time alone with God. Matthew 14:23 states, "After He had dismissed them, He went up on a mountainside by Himself to pray. When evening came, He was there alone." Mark 1:35 says, "Very early in the morning, while it was still dark, Jesus got up, left the house and went off to a solitary place, where He prayed." Luke 6:12–14 tells us, "One of those days Jesus went out to a mountainside to pray, and spent the night praying to God. When morning came, He called His disciples to Him and chose twelve of them, whom He also designated, Apostles."

In Luke 22:40–44 at the mount of Olives on the night that Jesus was betrayed, scripture tells us, "On reaching the place, He said to them, 'Pray that you will not fall into temptation.' He withdrew about a stone's throw beyond them, knelt down and prayed, 'Father, if you are willing, take this cup from me;

yet not my will, but yours be done.' An angel from heaven appeared to him and strengthened him. And being in anguish, he prayed more earnestly, and his sweat was like drops of blood falling to the ground."

A song by I. B. Sergei, titled "My God and I" has always been really inspirational to me in terms of relationships. The words read, "My God and I walk through the field together. We laugh and talk, as good friends should and do. We clasp our hands, our voices ring with laughter. My God and I, walk through the meadows hew."

Do you consider your relationship with God one of sharing, and communing, and of Him being your truest and deepest friend? Would you let Him in on your greatest fears, your deepest desires, your hopes, your sin, your trials and weaknesses? He already knows. Have you spent sufficient time alone with God to establish and maintain that relationship? Have you done the work to nurture that relationship by sharing experiences and learning about Him? He doesn't need it; after all, He is omniscient. You need it. You need to nurture your relationship with God. I need to nurture my relationship with God.

Relationships are frail, especially when people are involved. People let people down. That's why the only relationship that you can really count on is your relationship with God. The reality of our lives is that our relationship with God is not based on the strength of our congregation, or the heritage of our families, or even on any of our own strength or doing. It's based on the dedication, commitment, and love that we have for God.

We are workers in His vineyard, and it's our responsibility to get to know Him so that we can be pleasing as His servants. To those that are successful and understand Him to the point that we do what He desires, He allows us to become His heirs. Spending time alone with God is encouraging, releasing, relaxing, it cultivates within us the fruit of the Spirit; as found in Galatians 5:22, "love, joy, peace, patience, kindness, goodness, faithfulness, gentleness and self-control."

Spending time alone with God is the only way we are ever going to have that true, tight, bonding relationship that He wants. The kind of relationship that will cause Him to be glad to be with us. I can picture judgment when we will all stand before Christ. Will He be pleased with you? Will He be pleased with me? It will depend only and solely on our relationship with God. Our deep, committed, unbounded, completely honest relationship with our Creator. A relationship born of His grace through His Son, and strengthened for us through experience and time spent one-on-one, alone with God.

Then we can be assured that with a tear of love in His eyes, He will say "Welcome good and faithful servant (Matthew 25:23)."

Let me share a poem with you.

"I Care for You My God" by Dana H. Burnell

I fill my time; I fill my mind, with other busy
    thoughts;
I then begin to show myself as someone that I'm
    not.
It's not that I'm afraid or scared, to live so close
    to you.
It's just that I'm not good at it, and I know not
    what to do.
I try my best to keep your faith and friendship
    at the top.
But then life piles its cares on me, and friend-
    ship I've forgot.
I care, I care, I truly do, I wouldn't hurt you for
    the world.
It's just sometimes I get too busy, and my pa-
    tience comes unfurled.
It's then I tend to let you down; and then I tend
    to fail;
to work on our relationship; so great, so close,
    so frail.
And when I finally realize the error of my ways,
it seems we haven't talked at all, for many hours
    or days.
I love you with my heart of hearts, and every
    where would trod.
If I could just maintain my ways, my friend, my
    strength, my God.

Perhaps your relationship with God is faded and
you've realized that you aren't spending one on one

time alone with God. You aren't spending any time in prayer. Perhaps you have found that you have been spending less time and letting that relationship grow cold. You haven't done the necessary work to maintain that relationship. You can begin again, or work to make the relationship with God stronger. Because unlike people, God doesn't let us down. God is always standing with open arms for us to return to Him. Just like the father in the story of the prodigal son (Luke 15), God waits for us, even when we stray away from our relationship with Him. Luke 15:20 reads, "But while he was still a long way off, his father saw him and was filled with compassion for him; he ran to his son, threw his arms around him and kissed him." It says that the father ran to the son. God runs to us even more passionately when we grow weak. He wants us to return to Him.

Perhaps you've never made the commitment or the investment to spend time alone with God and get to know Him. Perhaps that relationship does not exist. Galatians 3:26–29 says, "You are all sons of God through faith in Christ Jesus, for all of you who were baptized into Christ have clothed yourselves with Christ. There is neither Jew nor Greek, slave nor free, male nor female, for you are all one in Christ Jesus. If you belong to Christ, then you are Abraham's seed, and heirs according to the promise." Christ said the second greatest commandment was to love our neighbors as ourselves. Remember what He said the greatest commandment was? To

Love the Lord your God with all of your heart, and all of your soul, and all of your mind (Matthew 22:37). God wants that relationship with us.

If you're not intimately involved with God I encourage you to pursue a relationship with Him today. Be baptized into His family, or strengthen your existing relationship.

Chapter 12

The Ones the Wolves Pulled Down

 I purposefully left this chapter towards the end of the book. As people we are called to obey Christ, to submit to His authority and to live lives consecrated to Him. God longs for us to obey the Gospel call and come to know Him fully through Christ Jesus. That's the invitation of God, to be saved through Christ. But salvation is not the end of our journey with Christ, it's the beginning. For the serious soul, faith cannot stop with our own conversion. There is work to do in God's kingdom and we are called to be workers.

Luke 28:18–20 reads, "Then Jesus came to them and said, 'All authority in heaven and on earth has been given to me. Therefore go and make disciples of all nations, baptizing them in the name of the

Father and of the Son and of the Holy Spirit, and teaching them to obey everything I have commanded you. And surely I am with you always, to the very end of the age.'"

This is called the great commission. Here we see Christ's last commandment as a man on earth. He told the Apostles, also His disciples, to go make disciples of all nations. He said to baptize them and teach them to do the same.

Disciple means follower, but it also means student. Jesus meant for this to be an everlasting business, this act of passing on the teaching and creation of disciples. As one becomes a disciple they have a responsibility to disciple others, who in turn disciple others . . . And so it goes.

We have a commandment from Christ to work to ensure that His Father's wishes are fulfilled; that no one is lost. That is a commandment that we need to take as seriously as any other commandments. Not doing so is a sin (James 4:17).

This chapter is about realizing that there are lost sheep amongst us, and that the true test of our faith is how we react to that fact. Do we run and hide, keep Christ to ourselves, or boldly proclaim the Gospel. We may be the only Jesus they ever meet.

In Matthew 10:16, Jesus was talking to His Disciples before He sent them out two-by-two in what we call the limited commission. He said "I am sending you out like sheep among wolves. Therefore be as shrewd as snakes and as innocent as doves."

What did Jesus mean that He was sending them out as sheep among wolves? He meant that He was sending them, His closest friends, and truest disciples out, and they would be extremely vulnerable to Satan. Satan was actually hunting for them, stalking, waiting to devour them. Satan, the wolf, was waiting to pull them down. There's not much comfort in that picture.

Let me share a few stories with you.

John

John was born in Cincinnati. His parents were upper-middle class and worked hard to provide for their three children. John didn't like to work. As he was growing up, he found that it was easier to shrug off responsibility than it was to have to put forth effort, so it was a constant battle for his parents to get him to clean his room or do his chores.

John graduated from high school and went on to become a finance clerk at the local bank. He had always had an affinity for numbers and so this job was right up his alley. He could get paid for doing something he was good at without having to put forth a lot of effort.

One day John was going to go to lunch with his co-workers but realized at the last minute that he had forgotten his wallet at home. John, in haste, decided to take $10 from the till and stop at home during lunch and get the money, replacing it right after lunch. During his haste at lunch, he forgot. When his till came up short at the end of the day, he was too embarrassed and ashamed to tell the truth, so he let it slide.

John found that money came easy after that. Any time he needed five or 10 dollars, he would "borrow" it from the bank. As time went on, he began taking larger amounts. One day, the bank security guards and two uniformed policemen escorted him from the bank to a waiting patrol car. He had been arrested. The bank kept track and John was convicted for embezzling almost 50,000 dollars from the bank.

Deborah

Deborah came from a poor family, but they had worked hard to make sure that they provided for her. She went to college, and it was there that she met the man of her dreams. His name was Bentley. He was a business major and was at the top of his class. They got married and Bentley got a job in a local business. Bentley was given the opportunity to become a trainer for his company. This meant a substantial pay increase, but it also meant that he would be on the road traveling about 60% of the time. He and Deborah discussed it and they decided that they would make the sacrifice of each others company for the money, at least for a couple of years.

Soon after Bentley started his new job, Deborah discovered that she didn't like being alone. When he was gone, she would hook up with her girl-friends and they would go to a movie, or out to dinner, or something. That kept her occupied. One night she couldn't find anyone to go out with, so she decided to go out alone. One thing led to an-other and she found herself sitting alone in a local bar. She had a couple of drinks and lost the better part of her judgment.

The next morning she awakened in a bed that was not her own, next to a man that was not her husband.

Timmy

Timmy was a good boy. He was bright and witty and had a great sense of humor. Everyone liked Timmy. One day, Timmy broke a lamp while play-ing in his grandmother's house. His two year old cousin was in the same room. Timmy thought that his cousin was so young that it could be an accident and he told a lie. He told the adults that his cousin broke the lamp. His cousin was young enough that they chalked it up as an accident and no one got in trouble. Timmy was never questioned because, after all, he was so likable.

Well, it wasn't long until he had his craft perfected and Timmy was telling lies all the time. He was able to do almost anything and get away with it, because he would lie his way out of it, so convincingly.

Timmy found that he had lied his way to the top of a successful company, and then lied his way to making that company successful. Tommy had fudged the figures a bit, and had kind of taken liberties with the press, and the Securities and Exchange Commission.

One day, Timmy was indicted for securities fraud and convicted to prison.

Frank

Frank was a big child. When he was three, he was almost a head taller then the other kids in his Sunday-school class. By about the age of five he was bossing kids around. He learned at a very early age that by being bigger he could get what he wanted. Sometimes the other children resisted. This made Frank so angry. Occasionally he would push them down.

As Frank got into Junior High and High School, his anger became a growing problem. He was in trouble frequently for fighting. He was known as one of the toughest kids in school and was not someone that you wanted on your bad side.

The summer after graduation, he had gone to the beach with a group of his friends. While they were there, Frank got into an argument with one of his friends. It escalated into a full-blown fight, and Frank ended up hitting his friend in the head. It must have been a lucky punch because his friend fell down, stopped fighting, and died, right there on the beach.

Frank was arrested for Murder, and even though his friends testified that he didn't mean to kill anyone, the judge looked at Frank's record. He saw that Frank had been a tough angry bully all his life, and determined that this was bound to happen eventually. Frank was sentenced to prison.

In prison, Frank's temper got the best of him again and he beat up on the wrong guy, a leader of a prison gang. The next day, the guards found Frank dead in his cell. He had been beaten to death.

Stacy

Stacy was a popular girl, a cheerleader, and a real likeable young lady. She graduated from high school with honors, and went on to a prestigious college, on a scholarship. Everyone was proud of Stacy.

Stacy was a very driven person with a type-A personality. She always wanted to be the best at what ever she did. She had a good heart and would never hurt anyone. She firmly believed that to be the best came from within. She knew that hard work was the only way to success.

Stacy had the idea that she wanted to graduate in three years, and then finish her Masters degree in the fourth year. She knew that this would give her a huge edge in the job market when she graduated. So, she took huge course loads to make her dream come true.

College was different than high school, and Stacy found that she had to really study hard to keep up. She was still getting straight A's though.

Stacy found that near the end of the year when they had final exams, she was incredibly tired and had too much studying to do to even allow herself enough time to sleep appropriately. She had heard of a product called no-doze, a safe caffeine substance that was like drinking several cups of coffee. Lots of students used it around this time of the year to stay awake and cram for tests.

Stacy started using no-doze. She found that with enough of it, she could stay awake for two-three days without having to lose time sleeping. Eventually, though the effects of this began to weaken. Stacy took summer school and things were still really hectic. She was on course for her early graduation, but found herself constantly getting tired, even with all the no-doze. One day she was discussing this with a classmate who told her that another friend had some pills that were like a super-no-doze. Stacy tried some.

During her second year of college, Stacy became a hard-core drug addict. She needed drugs to stay awake and she was always jumpy. She had lost a great deal of weight and her health was declining. By Christmas of her sophomore year, she succumbed to drugs and died of heart failure.

What do you see in common about all of these people?

- Each one of them started out with the same kind of life.
- They all started out with the ability to make choices.
- They all had opportunities that were before them.
- They all made decisions. They all made poor choices.
- They all stumbled.
- They all had excuses.
- They all were deceived by Satan to believe that something that was false.

- They were all ones that the wolves pulled down.

People have the ability every day to make choices. In Joshua, 24:14–15 it reads, "Now fear the LORD and serve him with all faithfulness. Throw away the gods your forefathers worshiped beyond the River and in Egypt, and serve the LORD. But if serving the LORD seems undesirable to you, then choose for yourselves this day whom you will serve, whether the gods your forefathers served beyond the river, or the gods of the Amorites, in whose land you are living. But as for me and my household, we will serve the LORD."

Here the Israelites had the choice to make, to serve God, or to serve others. Their families had served other gods, it was tradition. Some of them went on to serve other gods, and not the one true God. Some of them made poor choices. Some of them were taken down by the wolves.

Consider two questions. How many of your friends, or loved ones are making bad choices? How many of your co-workers or school mates, are being targeted by the wolves? How does that make you feel? What are you going to do about it?

In the first part of this chapter I want us to realize that it is really easy for those we know, that don't have a relationship with God, to make poor choices, poor decisions, and we have a responsibility, when we see it happening, to help.

Matthew 28:18–20 is often referred to as the "Great Commission." It reads, "Then Jesus came to them and said, 'All authority in heaven and on earth has been given to me. Therefore go and make disciples of all nations, baptizing them in the name of the Father and of the Son and of the Holy Spirit, and teaching them to obey everything I have commanded you. And surely I am with you always, to the very end of the age.'"

Here Christ is specifically speaking to the Apostles, but He tells them "teaching them to obey everything I have commanded you." This is God's message to spread the Gospel, and the term "everything" includes the part about "go and make disciples of all nations."

As believers we are commanded to share Christ with others. If you haven't told your neighbor about Christ, invited your co-workers to Church, invited your friends from school to your youth activities, you need to re-read and diligently study what we just read, the great commission. It's not a suggestion, it's a command. It's easy to say, "I'm too young, too old, too shy, too busy." Maybe it just hasn't been a priority.

First John 2:1–6 tells us, "We know that we have come to know Him if we obey His commands. The man who says, 'I know Him,' but does not do what He commands is a liar and the truth is not in him.

But if anyone obeys His word, God's love is truly made complete in him. This is how we know we are in Him: Whoever claims to live in Him must walk as Jesus did."

We are charged with the opportunity of telling those we spend time with about Christ. This ought to be a huge burden on us. If you don't feel for your neighbor you need to take some serious time and study what the Word of God says, because a good share of your friends and family are bound for an eternity, apart from God. This means that they are bound for HELL. Satan has got them firmly in his grasp, and in most cases, like the people we spoke about earlier he didn't even have to work at it.

Thankfully, just because they are in Satan's grasp, does not mean that they will always stay there. We have the ability and the obligation as disciples, Christians, the saved of God, to tell our neighbors about Christ, and to work and fight so that they are not the ones the wolves pull down.

The message from the first part of this chapter is this: Our friends, our loved ones, our neighbors, are being taken down every day by Satan's wolves. Most don't even put up a fight. As Christians, we should be moved by that into action. Out of our Christian love we should have hearts that are broken for the lost.

The second part of this chapter invokes another question: How are we different?

When are we capable of making poor choices and stumbling and falling down a path that will lead to destruction? How many of us have problems with greed, or lust, or envy, or pride, or other things that could easily cause us to make the same kinds of poor decisions that would lead us away from God. I would submit that we are all in the same shape. We are all capable of making poor choices and walking away from our relationship with God (Hebrews 6:6).

But there are three very distinct differences for a Christian when you're talking about this being pulled down by the wolves.

The first is that we are covered by the Blood of Christ. Second Peter 15:9 reads, "For this very reason, make every effort to add to your faith goodness; and to goodness, knowledge; and to knowledge, self-control; and to self-control, perseverance; and to perseverance, godliness; and to godliness, brotherly kindness; and to brotherly kindness, love. For if you possess these qualities in increasing measure, they will keep you from being ineffective and unproductive in your knowledge of our Lord Jesus Christ. But if anyone does not have them, he is nearsighted and blind, and has forgotten that he has been cleansed from his past sins."

Our sins are forgiven when we are baptized and cleansed by the Blood of Christ. Our sins are forgiven and the burden of those sins lifted from us so that without that load of sin we may be stronger to fight against the temptations that befall us.

The second is that we are strengthened by the Holy Spirit. In Acts 2:38 it says, "Peter replied, 'Repent and be baptized, every one of you, in the name of Jesus Christ for the forgiveness of your sins. And you will receive the gift of the Holy Spirit.'"

The Spirit was sent to live in the lives of believers, strengthening them, giving them a greater sense of right and wrong, helping them to make wise choices and resist the wolves. John 16:13–15 shows us this. It reads, "But when he, the Spirit of truth, comes, he will guide you into all truth. He will not speak on his own; he will speak only what he hears, and he will tell you what is yet to come. He will bring glory to me by taking from what is mine and making it known to you. All that belongs to the Father is mine. That is why I said the Spirit will take from what is mine and make it known to you."

The third difference is that we are tracked more intensely by the wolves. It's Satan's desire to win the entire world, and Gods desire that none be lost. It is indeed a battle. For those that have not put on Christ, how hard does Satan have to work? He doesn't! He's already got them and they don't even know it! So Satan is really after those that are resisting him and doing Gods will.

But just like the people that we talked about before, none of them started out evil, none of them started out wanting to sin. None of them wanted to be outside of God. None of them planned to fall into the snares of temptation and end up a slave of the evil one. They all just stumbled. They all fell. And Satan wasn't even really working at it.

Satan is breathing down our necks waiting for us to make a mistake and stumble. How many of you can feel the power of Satan around you? How many of you know that he is alive and working diligently to cause you to fall? Satan wants you to become one of the ones that the wolves pulled down.

First John 1:8–10 tells us, "If we claim to be without sin, we deceive ourselves and the truth is not in us. If we confess our sins, He is faithful and just and will forgive us our sins and purify us from all unrighteousness. If we claim we have not sinned, we make Him out to be a liar and His word has no place in our lives."

We are all sinners, capable of making poor decisions every day. Have you made a poor decision today, this week, this month, this year?

But what does it mean to be without sin, what does it mean to do God's will? James 1:13–15 says, "When tempted, no one should say, 'God is tempting me.' For God cannot be tempted by evil, nor does He tempt anyone; but each one is tempted when, by his own evil desire, he is dragged away and enticed. Then, after desire has conceived, it gives birth to sin; and sin, when it is full-grown, gives birth to death."

Doing God's will means first to understand the battle that we are in. We are fighting for our lives, our spiritual lives. It doesn't get any tougher. To win, we need to recognize the battle, see our sin openly and honestly, and change to do God's will.

Matthew 5:39–48 says, "But I tell you, do not resist an evil person. If someone strikes you on the right cheek, turn to him the other also. And if someone wants to sue you and take your tunic, let him have your cloak as well. If someone forces you to go one mile, go with him two miles. Give to the one who asks you, and do not turn away from the one who wants to borrow from you. You have heard that it was said, `Love your neighbor and hate your enemy.' But I tell you: Love your enemies and pray for those who persecute you, that you may be sons of your Father in heaven. He causes his sun to rise on the evil and the good, and sends rain on the righteous and the unrighteous. If you love those who love you, what reward will you get? Are not even the tax collectors doing that? And if you greet only your brothers, what are you doing more than others? Do not even pagans do that? Be perfect, therefore, as your heavenly Father is perfect."

Doing God's will means love without measure for all. It's more than just being a good person. It's about raising the bar continually in your walk towards Christian maturity. It's constantly and consistently asking more of yourself for God. It's giving the first fruits of your life, your money, your time, your love. It's pressing on towards the goal.

God gives us the tools to stand firm in our faith. Ephesians 6:10–18 describes it. "Finally, be strong in the Lord and in his mighty power. Put on the full armor of God so that you can take your stand against the devil's schemes. For our struggle is not against flesh and blood, but against the rulers, against the authorities, against the powers of this dark world and against the spiritual forces of evil in the heavenly realms. Therefore put on the full armor of God, so that when the day of evil comes, you may be able to stand your ground, and after you have done everything, to stand. Stand firm then, with the belt of truth buckled around your waist, with the breastplate of righteousness in place, and with your feet fitted with the readiness that comes from the gospel of peace. In addition to all this, take up the shield of faith, with which you can extinguish all the flaming arrows of the evil one. Take the helmet of salvation and the sword of the Spirit, which is the word of God. And pray in the Spirit on all occasions with all kinds of prayers and requests. With this in mind, be alert and always keep on praying for all the saints."

Let me share a poem with you.

"Running From the Wolves" by Dana H. Burnell

My friends, the sheep, are feeding in the valley
    of the sin.
They do not have a shepherd, just a fence to keep
    them in.
They never even saw the wolves as their lives
    were torn away.
They simply fell without a fight, succumbing as
    the prey.

They didn't even seem to see, that they were
    being stalked.
They couldn't see them coming, from they path
    way where they walked.
They fell right there upon the path, and breathed
    a breath, their last,
and quickly, very quickly, their bleating voices
    faded fast.

I am a deer, a fast one, blessed by God with speed
    and sight.
When I see the wolves come near me, a run fast
    with all my might.
When I hear their voices howling, I recognize
    their sound,

and I work hard to avoid them, I'm afraid when
    they're around.

I've a friend who died last Friday, sweetest sheep,
    he didn't see,
that the wolves had come a running, after him
    and after me.
Lord I pray I'm always leery, on my guard with
    sight and sound,
so I'll never fall to Satan, and the wolves won't
    pull me down.

I exhort you to Study God's word. Pray earnestly, and live the Gospel to which you were called. The wolves of Satan are pulling down people right and left and they are zeroing in on God's elect. With God's love, we don't need to be afraid. But we do need to be aware.

It doesn't matter whether you are being held lovingly in the hand of God, or held in the grasp of Satan, so long as there is breath in you, you can make choices that change your destiny, either way. The best of Christians can choose to walk away from God, and the worst of sinners can turn their lives around through Christ.

If you are a Christian and you are making poor choices, letting yourself be entrapped by the desires of the world, and perhaps stretching the distance between your hand and Gods, you can fix that today. You're being actively hunted, and Satan wants to win. Seek prayers, love, and strength from your Christian family and from God.

If you're not a Christian chances are, the wolves either have you or are really close. Protect yourself with the armor of God and He will show you the way. Become a part of God's army, by choice, not Satan's victim because of ignorance.

Chapter 13

How Long?

Let me share a story with you.

When I was in college I was a computer science major. Although a lot of my coursework was based on writing computer programs I still had tests in every class. The tests that were most important to my grades were either the mid-term exams or the final exams. These two tests generally were great barometers to tell you what kind of a grade you currently held, or what kind of a grade you were going to get for the course.

Like most students there were courses that came really easy for me. These were classes where I could almost be certain that I would get an A or B for a grade. These courses were usually were met with ambition and excitement and were easy to excel in. The courses that didn't come so easy were the courses where either I didn't really grasp the material, or I didn't like the content of the course. In those courses I really needed to study harder, work more, and put more effort into learning the material.

One such course was a programming course. I didn't really grasp the material and I was busy with other courses, so I didn't spend much time or effort learning the material for this particular course. When it came time for the final exam, I was unprepared and had to cram for the test. For those that may be wondering, "cram" means to learn in an evening or a weekend what you should have learned during the semester. It means "cramming" the material into your head.

So I stayed up most of the night reviewing the material from the course in an effort to learn in a few short hours what I had neglected to learn in an entire semester. The test was at 8:00 in the morning and was a two hour test. At about 4:30 am I was finally so exhausted that I was ready to take what ever grade I got on the test and knew that I was as "ready as I'd ever be" considering the circumstances. So I laid down for an hour or two of much needed sleep.

I woke up the next morning at about 8:45. Yikes! I was already 45 minutes late for the start of my two hour test. I rushed around like a mad man and made it to school to take the test. I got there with 50 minutes left. I ripped my way through the test, and finished on time. However when grades came out I got a D on the final exam, a D in the course and had to repeat the course the next semester.

The problem was that I wasn't prepared, I wasn't ready. I had procrastinated and tried to play catch up when it became urgent to do so. Talk about a combination of stress and lack of sense. I knew what to do. I knew what was coming, but I waited until the end. And I waited too long.

This chapter is about looking at the message of the Gospel and understanding the urgency of its message, and the seriousness of its call for preparation.

In First Thessalonians 4:16–18 we read, "For the Lord himself will come down from heaven, with a loud command, with the voice of the archangel and with the trumpet call of God, and the dead in Christ will rise first. After that, we who are still alive and are left will be caught up together with them in the clouds to meet the Lord in the air. And so we will be with the Lord forever. Therefore encourage each other with these words." It's clear that the Lord is going to return.

Continuing on in chapter five, verses 1–6 it reads, "Now, brothers, about times and dates we do not need to write to you, for you know very well that the day of the Lord will come like a thief in the night. While people are saying, 'Peace and safety,' destruction will come on them suddenly, as labor pains on a pregnant woman, and they will not escape. But you, brothers, are not in darkness so that this day should surprise you like a thief. You are all sons of the light and sons of the day. We do not belong to the night or to the darkness. So then, let us not be like others, who are asleep, but let us be alert and self-controlled." It's clear that Christ is coming again, that no one knows when, and that we need to be prepared at all times.

Second Thessalonians 1:5–10 teaches, "All this is evidence that God's judgment is right, and as a result you will be counted worthy of the kingdom of God, for which you are suffering. God is just: He will pay back trouble to those who trouble you and give relief to you who are troubled, and to us as well. This will happen when the Lord Jesus is revealed from heaven in blazing fire with his powerful angels. He will punish those who do not know God and do not obey the gospel of our Lord Jesus. They will be punished with everlasting destruction and shut out from the presence of the Lord and from the majesty of his power on the day he comes to be glorified in his holy people and to be marveled at among all those who have believed. This includes you, because you believed our testimony to you."

Hebrews 9:27–28 shows us, "Just as man is destined to die once, and after that to face judgment, so Christ was sacrificed once to take away the sins of many people; and he will appear a second time, not to bear sin, but to bring salvation to those who are waiting for him."

These passages clearly demonstrate a message that Jesus is going to return and that both the living and the dead will be judged by whether they obeyed the Gospel.

We know that there is a point at which either we are going to physically die, or Christ is going to return. Just like my programming course, we know the final exam is scheduled. We understand the situation, and have all the preparatory material at our fingertips. It's up to us whether we want to prepare or not.

The reason that I wanted to write this chapter is because I fear that we don't take the urgency of the Gospel seriously. We live our own lives as though we have all the time in the world to get serious about our faith, and put the "Great Commission" (Matthew 28:18–20) at the bottom of our "to-do" list.

I want to share two thoughts with you in this chapter. The first is this: God has called us to live a righteous life, and explained to us in detail what that means. He has described for us both the reward for doing His will, and the punishment for not doing it.

What does it mean to live righteously? Galatians 5:19–21 tells us, "The acts of the sinful nature are obvious: sexual immorality, impurity and debauchery; idolatry and witchcraft; hatred, discord, jealousy, fits of rage, selfish ambition, dissensions, factions and envy; drunkenness, orgies, and the like. I warn you, as I did before, that those who live like this will not inherit the kingdom of God."

The phrase, "And the like," changes the passage above from a checklist to a way of living. It means anything like hatred; anything like idolatry; anything like sexual immorality. That verse says, "Those who live like this will not inherit the kingdom of God."

Obviously, righteous living means abstaining from sinful behavior, but it's more than that. Romans 1:17 tells us "For in the gospel a righteousness from God is revealed, a righteousness that is by faith from first to last just as it is written: 'The righteous will live by faith.'"

Righteous living means that we abstain from evil behavior BECAUSE we have faith that the Gospel is true, and that Jesus Christ is going to come again and bring the righteous with Him to eternity (Matthew 25:46).

Often times we fail to live righteously because sin lulls us into believing that living on the edge of our faith is enough. We tell ourselves, "I'm really a good person, and God knows that." "Yeah, I do have a few things I need to change but I'll get to it some day, and if I don't well God's a loving God, right?" We wait until we feel we are ready to change. And we live life on the edge of the fence. We dabble a little here and there in things that are "borderline" activities, or "gray areas" in the Bible.

We tell a little white lie here, or give a not completely told truth there. We buy a lottery ticket now and then "to help the parks department" or whomever that money goes to. We gossip a little about a brother or sister, or we allow ourselves to be a little jealous or little angry for a little while. We lust a little and write it off by saying, "look but don't touch." We forsake the assembly for our favorite sporting event. And we have a little outburst when we fail to control our temper. It sounds to me as though all of these things fall into the category of "and the like" (Galatians 5:21).

And we do this to ourselves at the expense of the peace that God wants us to have. Philippians chapter four tells us in verses 4–7, "Rejoice in the Lord always. I will say it again: Rejoice! Let your gentleness be evident to all. The Lord is near. Do not be anxious about anything, but in everything, by prayer and petition, with thanksgiving, present your requests to God. And the peace of God, which transcends all understanding, will guard your hearts and your minds in Christ Jesus."

But all the blame does not lie on us. First Peter 5:8–9 tells us, "Be self-controlled and alert. Your enemy the devil prowls around like a roaring lion looking for someone to devour. Resist him, standing firm in the faith, because you know that your brothers throughout the world are undergoing the same kind of sufferings." Satan is looking for a way to lead us astray and he is a pretty formidable foe.

There are two main keys to empowering ourselves to live righteous lives. These are to know God, and to be known by each other.

In Matthew 22: 37 Jesus tells us that the greatest command is to "Love the Lord your God with all your heart and with all your soul and with all your mind." In John 14:21 Jesus tells us, "Whoever has my commands and obeys them, he is the one who loves me. He who loves me will be loved by my Father, and I too will love him and show myself to him." If the greatest command is to love God with everything we have, and the demonstration of that love is to obey His commands, we need to be doing what He commands. How do we know what His commands are?

In John 7:17, Jesus says, "If anyone chooses to do God's will, he will find out whether my teaching comes from God or whether I speak on my own." Read that sentence again. The Son of God tells us "If anyone chooses to do God's will, he will find out whether my teaching comes from God or whether I speak on my own." Second Timothy 3:16 tells us that, "All Scripture is God-breathed and is useful for teaching, rebuking, correcting and training in righteousness, so that the man of God may be thoroughly equipped for every good work."

Daily Bible reading is the only way to establish a deep understanding of God. If we really love God we'll want to spend time daily getting to know Him better. And in fact we're commanded to do it. Second Timothy 2:25 says, "Do your best to present yourself to God as one approved, a workman who does not need to be ashamed and who correctly handles the word of truth."

The second way to empower us to live righteous lives is to make sure that we are intimately involved in each others lives.

Hebrews 3:13 tells us, "But encourage one another daily, as long as it is called Today, so that none of you may be hardened by sin's deceitfulness." We don't necessarily want people involved in our lives, right? They may see some things that are not really what they should be and we might be embarrassed.

Heaven forbid that we look less than our Sunday best in front of our Church family. But that's exactly the message of Hebrews 3:13, to hold each other accountable so that we can ensure that we are living the righteous lives that God has called us to.

I heard a preacher say one time that "we need to be transparent to each other." We need to look exactly as we are in front of our Church family. We need to look exactly the same in front of our Church family as we do in front of God.

Scripture tells us that we need to confess our faults to one another (James 5:16), encourage one another (Hebrews 10:24), edify each other (Romans 14:18), bear one another's burdens (Galatians 6:2). The way for us to ensure that we are headed towards the narrow gate is to be involved in each others lives to the point that we are transparent to each other.

It's hard to have the devil hiding in your closet when you're living in a glass house.

How would you feel about tossing copies of your house keys to your Christian brothers and sisters and tell them, "drop by any time." They could come by when you're not at your best. Remember, Jesus has the house keys and He's going to drop by anytime. That's part of the urgent message of the Gospel.

As we read in Ecclesiastes 4:9–12, "Two are better than one, because they have a good return for their work: If one falls down, his friend can help him up. But pity the man who falls and has no one to help him up! Also, if two lie down together, they will keep warm. But how can one keep warm alone? Though one may be overpowered, two can defend themselves. A cord of three strands is not quickly broken."

We need to be accountable. It's not so much that we need to be accountable TO each other. We need to be accountable FOR each other. In turn that leads us to bear each others burdens and to share each others joys.

Let me share a prayer with you.

My Lord I want to be the person that you've called me to be. I want to live for you wholeheartedly and with all the passion I can muster. Father I want to know you in a way that only we can share. I want to understand you intimately so that I can understand what you want from me. I want to have your Word emblazoned in my heart so that all of my behavior and thoughts can be filtered through the looking glass of your will.

Lord, I also want to help my Christian family and lean on them in return. I want to have relationships where I can help lift my family up, and help to guide them through your word to be the people you have called us to be. I want to be able to be a shoulder to cry on, or a heart to pour out to. I want to be a sounding board for life's questions and a loudspeaker for praises.

Lord I need to have my Christian family there when I need a hand. I sometimes need course corrections or have a burden that I need to share. I pray that they can be there for me and that I can be humble enough to ask for help. I also need my family to share in the blessings you bestow on me. I am so blessed by you Father that I need to share my overflowing cup with others.

Thank you Lord for allowing me to bring this to you, and I pray that I live to be the person you desire, to know you as my Lord and friend, and to relish in the giving and receiving of the blessings of the saved. You are my Lord and my God. Amen.

Living a righteous life means having the faith necessary to live for God. It means using that faith to get to know Him through His Word. It means being there for, and depending on your Christian family in a way that promotes the love of God, and the accountability that we need for each other.

We are called to live righteously and the lives that we live now are our only chance to do so. We need to make sure that we are living for God, and staying the course. If your not living as you know you should, the question is, "How long will you wait?"

The second thought I want to share with you from this chapter is this: What about those around us?

Second Peter 3:9 says, "The Lord is not slow in keeping his promise, as some understand slowness. He is patient with you, not wanting anyone to perish, but everyone to come to repentance." God wants all men and women everywhere to repent and be baptized, living righteous lives for Him. In fact He loved the world so much that in John 3:16–17 He tells us, "For God so loved the world that he gave his one and only Son, that whoever believes in him shall not perish but have eternal life. For God did not send his Son into the world to condemn the world, but to save the world through Him." Luke 19:10 tells us, "For the Son of Man came to seek and to save what was lost."

It's clear that God doesn't want anyone to be lost. Remember back in First John 2:6 it said, "Whoever claims to live in him must walk as Jesus did." I think that means that we must live like we don't want any to be lost as well.

In Mark 16:15–16 Jesus tells His disciples, "Go into all the world and preach the good news to all creation. Whoever believes and is baptized will be saved, but whoever does not believe will be condemned." We have an obligation to bring the Gospel of Christ to the lost of the world. It's not a choice, it's a commandment.

We are a people of excuses though. We say things like, "Oh I'm not blessed with the gift of evangelism." "I'm not really a people person." First Timothy 3:16 tells us that Scripture thoroughly prepares us for all good work.

So we say things like, "Well, I don't want to risk driving my family away from me if I tell them about Jesus." Jesus said in Matthew 10:34–39, "Do not suppose that I have come to bring peace to the earth. I did not come to bring peace, but a sword. For I have come to turn a man against his father, a daughter against her mother, a daughter-in-law against her mother-in-law, a man's enemies will be the members of his own household. Anyone who loves his father or mother more than me is not worthy of me; anyone who loves his son or daughter more than me is not worthy of me; and anyone who does not take his cross and follow me is not worthy of me. Whoever finds his life will lose it, and whoever loses his life for my sake will find it." No matter how we try to squirm, we can't escape the fact that we are commanded to share the Gospel with those around us.

Once we understand our calling we have to ask, "Who are those lost and how do we reach out to them?" The first thing we need to understand is that a life with Christ is not a part-time job. We're either committed or we're not. Jesus said in Luke 11:23, "He who is not with me is against me, and he who does not gather with me, scatters." Revelation 3:14 tells us, "To the angel of the church in Laodicea write: These are the words of the Amen, the faithful and true witness, the ruler of God's creation. I know your deeds, that you are neither cold nor hot. I wish you were either one or the other! So, because you are lukewarm—neither hot nor cold—I am about to spit you out of my mouth." In Matthew 22: 37 Jesus tells us that the greatest command is to "Love the Lord your God with all your heart and with all your soul and with all your mind." It's not a part time job, and we're either living it all day every day or we're fooling ourselves. Choosing a life with Christ is a serious and total commitment that takes serious diligence to keep it on the narrow road.

Matthew 13:1–9 tells us, "That same day Jesus went out of the house and sat by the lake. Such large crowds gathered around him that he got into a boat and sat in it, while all the people stood on the shore. Then he told them many things in parables, saying: 'A farmer went out to sow his seed. As he was scattering the seed, some fell along the path, and the birds came and ate it up. Some fell on rocky places, where it did not have much soil. It sprang up quickly, because the soil was shallow. But when the sun came up, the plants were scorched, and they withered because they had no root. Other seed fell among thorns, which grew up and choked the plants. Still other seed fell on good soil, where it produced a crop—a hundred, sixty or thirty times what was sown. He who has ears, let him hear.'"

We need to be spreading seed everywhere, because we don't know what the soil is that we're working with. We can't judge a person's heart and we can't make assumptions based on our own personal biases. Sometimes we do that though. We say to ourselves, "they won't listen to me" or "I wouldn't know how to even start the conversation" or "how do I even relate to them?"

In verse's 18–23 Jesus explains the parable. It reads, "Listen then to what the parable of the sower means: When anyone hears the message about the kingdom and does not understand it, the evil one comes and snatches away what was sown in his heart. This is the seed sown along the path. The one who received the seed that fell on rocky places is the man who hears the word and at once receives it with joy. But since he has no root, he lasts only a short time. When trouble or persecution comes because of the word, he quickly falls away. The one who received the seed that fell among the thorns is the man who hears the word, but the worries of this life and the deceitfulness of wealth choke it, making it unfruitful. But the one who received the seed that fell on good

soil is the man who hears the word and under-
stands it. He produces a crop, yielding a hundred,
sixty or thirty times what was sown."

In this parable we see four types of soil. In three
of those four cases the Word was received. In one
case it was not. In the case of the seed sown along
the path, it didn't have time to germinate before it
was overtaken by evil. In the case of the seed that
produced a crop, it's apparent that the seed took
hold and flourished. In the other two cases, though,
these are people that we would consider saved, at
some point. They accepted the Word and began to
grow. But they were overtaken by sin.

Scripture is full of examples that show us that
it's possible that we may fall away from our faith.
"Jesus replied, 'No one who puts his hand to the
plow and looks back is fit for service in the king-
dom of God.' (Luke 10:62)." "Watch out that you
do not lose what you have worked for, but that you
may be rewarded fully (Second John 1:8)." "If any-
one does not remain in me, he is like a branch that
is thrown away and withers; such branches are
picked up, thrown into the fire and burned (John
15:6)." "If we deliberately keep on sinning after we
have received the knowledge of the truth, no sacri-
fice for sins is left, but only a fearful expectation of
judgment and of raging fire that will consume the
enemies of God (Hebrews 10:26–27)." "The Spirit
clearly says that in later times some will abandon

From Grace to Eternity

the faith and follow deceiving spirits and things taught by demons (First Timothy 4:1)."

Scripture is also full of examples of the saved that become lost. In Luke 15:4–10 Jesus says, "Suppose one of you has a hundred sheep and loses one of them. Does he not leave the ninety-nine in the open country and go after the lost sheep until he finds it? And when he finds it, he joyfully puts it on his shoulders and goes home. Then he calls his friends and neighbors together and says, 'Rejoice with me; I have found my lost sheep.' I tell you that in the same way there will be more rejoicing in heaven over one sinner who repents than over ninety-nine righteous persons who do not need to repent. Or suppose a woman has ten silver coins and loses one. Does she not light a lamp, sweep the house and search carefully until she finds it? And when she finds it, she calls her friends and neighbors together and says, 'Rejoice with me; I have found my lost coin.' In the same way, I tell you, there is rejoicing in the presence of the angels of God over one sinner who repents."

The sheep already belonged to the shepherd, but it was lost. The coin already belonged to the woman, but it was lost. These examples are not talking about people that never heard, they are talking about people that heard and were united by faith into God grace through baptism into our Lord Jesus Christ. These are people that were saved but had fallen away.

Matthew 18:12–14 tells another account of the story of the lost sheep. It reads, "What do you think? If a man owns a hundred sheep, and one of them wanders away, will he not leave the ninety-nine on the hills and go to look for the one that wandered off? And if he finds it, I tell you the truth, he is happier about that one sheep than about the ninety-nine that did not wander off. In the same way your Father in heaven is not willing that any of these little ones should be lost."

But continuing in the same passage it follows with this: "If your brother sins against you, go and show him his fault, just between the two of you. If he listens to you, you have won your brother over. But if he will not listen, take one or two others along, so that 'every matter may be established by the testimony of two or three witnesses.' If he refuses to listen to them, tell it to the church; and if he refuses to listen even to the church, treat him as you would a pagan or a tax collector."

We have an obligation as Christians to help our fallen brother or sister to find their way back to God. Galatians 6:1–2 tells us, "Brothers, if someone is caught in a sin, you who are spiritual should restore him gently. But watch yourself, or you also may be tempted. Carry each other's burdens, and in this way you will fulfill the law of Christ." James 5:19–20 says, "My brothers, if one of you should wander from the truth and someone should bring him back, remember this: Whoever turns a sinner from the error of his way will save him from death and cover over a multitude of sins." Hebrews 3:12–13 reminds us, "See to it, brothers, that none of you has a sinful, unbelieving heart that turns away from the living God. But encourage one another daily, as long as it is called Today, so that none of you may be hardened by sin's deceitfulness."

The story of the Prodigal son was not strictly about the son, it was also about the Father and the angry Brother. In Luke 15:28–32 it says, "The older brother became angry and refused to go in. So his father went out and pleaded with him. But he answered his father, 'Look! All these years I've been slaving for you and never disobeyed your orders. Yet you never gave me even a young goat so I could celebrate with my friends. But when this son of yours who has squandered your property with prostitutes comes home, you kill the fattened calf for him!' 'My son,' the father said, 'you are always with me, and everything I have is yours. But we had to celebrate and be glad, because this brother of yours was dead and is alive again; he was lost and is found.'"

We need to rejoice with our brothers and sisters that have found their way home again, just as much as we do with those new brothers and sisters that are first beginning their walk with Christ.

Again, this is a call to involvement in each others lives. We need to not only be involved so that we keep each other on the right track, but that when we stray we bring each other back to the right track. That's how we turn a sinner from the error of his ways, that's how we bear one another's burdens.

If we truly are to have hearts that are broken for the lost, we need to reach out to them, but not only to the overtly lost, but also to the wayward brother or sister as well.

The Gospel message, the Word of God, the Scriptures of the New Testament teach a message of love and hope for the believer, dread and damnation for the unbeliever. It contains and unmistakable sense of urgency for all of us.

We know what we need to do, but we wait. We wait on checking our own behavior. We wait on getting involved in each others lives. We wait on studying Gods Word. We wait on helping our neighbor find God, or helping our brothers or sisters maintain their walk. We wait and wait and wait and wait. How long will be too long?

Let me share a poem with you.

"Righteousness For All" by Dana H. Burnell

I try to live my life for God in all the things I do.
I try to understand His will and let His light
    shine through.

I pray I get to know Him through the study of
    His Word
And that I can rightly handle it, for it is a two
    edged sword.

I pray I am transparent, to the family of the Lord.
I pray that they can see my faults and guide me
    towards His Word.
I pray that I can help them too, a brother fighting
    strong,
And shoulder next to shoulder we can take the
    battle on.

I pray I have within my heart, a burden for the
    lost.
And that it spurs me onward, to introduce them
to the cross.
So when I stand before the Lord, and he ushers
    me in,
You're all right there beside me, clothed with
Christ, and free from sin.

We need to be diligent for ourselves and for those
around us. Jesus reminds us that few are righteous.
In Luke 17:26–29 He says, "Just as it was in the
days of Noah, so also will it be in the days of the
Son of Man. People were eating, drinking, marrying
and being given in marriage up to the day Noah en-
tered the ark. Then the flood came and destroyed
them all. It was the same in the days of Lot. People
were eating and drinking, buying and selling, plant-
ing and building. But the day Lot left Sodom, fire

and sulfur rained down from heaven and destroyed them all."

Jesus is predicting the fact that many will choose not to come to repentance and not to accept God's gift of grace. In Matthew 7:13–14 we see Him mention this again. It reads, "Enter through the narrow gate. For wide is the gate and broad is the road that leads to destruction, and many enter through it. But small is the gate and narrow the road that leads to life, and only a few find it."

Let me share a story with you.

Clyde and Jeff Sampson were businessmen. They each had earned an MBA from a prestigious school and upon graduation they opened an appliance store. This was not just another appliance store. It was the biggest store in the tri-county area. Sampson's Appliances carried more models and a larger stock of appliances than almost all the rest of their competitors combined. Clyde and Jeff worked hard to make this store profitable.

After a few years of working together they had a major disagreement. They had disagreed before, but never to this extent. The problem was that Clyde wanted to start financing sales for people, and collecting monthly payments and an interest amount. He saw it as another revenue source and thought that it was a great idea. Jeff disagreed and thought that it would be another issue to deal with and believed that it would bring a great amount of financial risk. He argued that people wouldn't pay their payments and that after having to pay a charge to collect. Sampson's would be out the sale, the collection amount, and have a worthless used appliance to deal with.

The disagreement became so severe that Jeff left the business. He sold his share to Clyde for a reasonable price, but he was so angered by the whole affair that he vowed never to speak to Clyde again.

Years passed and Jeff decided that it was silly to keep this distance between he and his brother Clyde. So he decided to have Clyde and his wife over for dinner the next week. He called Clyde's wife and prepared the meeting. She was delighted to see that the brothers were going to get together again.

Jeff got busy with his plan. He did the shopping and bought a roast, along with all the fixings. Jeff was up late the evening before the big day getting everything prepared. When he lay down to sleep, he noticed a dull ache in his left arm. He brushed it off as old age and rolled over on his right side to sleep. Jeff never woke up. He died that night of a heart attack.

Jeff wanted to fix the broken relationship with his brother Clyde. He let it go for months and years. Finally he decided to do something about it. But Jeff waited too long. He never got the chance to say the things he wanted to say, give the hug he'd been longing to give, and patch the brotherhood that had so long been broken. When death comes, you don't get a second chance.

If you're not sure of your salvation, you need to fix that today. If you don't know Christ, you need to know Him. In Acts 2:38 the people realized their lost state and Peter told them to be baptized. If you don't know Christ you need to be immersed into His death through baptism. If you're already a member of His family but you find yourself apart from God, living in that area where you're dabbling in sin. God says you're lost. Repair your relationship. Come to know Him through His Word. Let people into your life, ask for accountability, and let the Love of Christ flow through your Christian family. In either case you need to ask yourself, "How long are you going to wait?" "How long is too long?"

If you are sure that your life is on track, consider the people around you. Are you reaching out to them? Have they never heard? Have they fallen away? Can you even tell the difference? The gate is narrow that leads to destruction and few are those who find it. Your friends, family, co-workers, your wayward brother or sister, don't know the way to the narrow gate. You may have been in the field with him or her for a long time. You need to ask yourself the question, "How long are you going to wait?" "How long is too long?"

Hebrews 12: verses one and two say, "Therefore, since we are surrounded by such a great cloud of witnesses, let us throw off everything that hinders and the sin that so easily entangles, and let us run with perseverance the race marked out for us. Let us fix our eyes on Jesus, the author and perfecter of our faith, who for the joy set before him endured the cross, scorning its shame, and sat down at the right hand of the throne of God."

Epilogue

As I said in the beginning of this book, I am not a preacher, an eloquent public speaker or an inspirational writer. I am simply a student of God. I've prayed over this book many times. The week before I sent it to the publisher I asked all my editors to pray about it. The night that I sent it to the publisher my wife and I prayed over it.

This book may have had content that helped you to begin your walk with God. If this is the case, Hallelujah! This book may have had content that helped you grow stronger in your walk with God. If this is the case, Hallelujah! This book may have helped charge your heart into action to help God win a lost soul, or strengthen a brother or sister. If this is the case, Hallelujah!

Or perhaps this book only made you think. Amen! The first step of looking for God is consideration of our current state. The first step of living for God is desiring to know what He wants from our lives. The first step of loving like Jesus loved is to consider the lost. This is the journey from Grace to Eternity. If this book made you think, then it has had a purpose.

As I draw this work to a close, I am so thankful that God saw fit to allow me to write the words I have written, and I have tearfully and prayerfully worked to keep them in accordance with His Word. This book is a work of love, dedication, and commitment to my Lord. It is to Him that this book is dedicated. It is to Him that any glory this work engenders needs to be given. It is with Him that I want to be eternally.

Make no mistake; Jesus Christ is my Lord and my Savior. He is the Son of God, the great I AM. I am nothing without Him, and I am a priest, a child of God, a brother of Jesus, with Him.

If you need to put on Christ in baptism, if you want to give your life to God, if you want to live for Jesus, do something about it now. God is knocking on your door, answer quickly before you hear him no more.

My prayer for you is this:

Epilogue

Father God, bless all who have read this work. Bless them Father so that they may somehow see you, and see themselves. Father let the saved see themselves as messengers of yours, called to live a holy life. Let the saved be empowered to overcome temptation and sin. Let the saved be energized to reach out to the lost and the lukewarm. Father, bless the saved with the right things to say, the right opportunities, the right heart, to do your work and your will.

Father, bless the seeking. Bless those that are earnestly looking for something more fulfilling than the words of the world. Bless them Father that their eyes will be opened and their feet set on a path towards you. Embrace them Father as they follow your will, and let us as brethren embrace them with a love like yours.

Father, bless those that are empowered and emboldened by your Word. Bless those that are on fire for your purpose. Help us all Father to have hearts broken for the lost and the lukewarm. You way, Father, is the only way and I pray that many find it. I pray that many live it. I pray that many share it. To God be the Glory! Amen.

To order additional copies of

Have your credit card ready and call:

1-877-421-READ (7323)

or please visit our web site at
www.pleasantword.com

Also available at: www.amazon.com

Printed in the United States
20406LVS00001B/86

9 781414 100630